Professional Learning Conversations: Challenges in Using Evidence for Improvement

D1600500

Professional Learning and Development in Schools and Higher Education

Volume 1

Series Editors

Christopher Day
School of Education, University of Nottingham, UK
Judyth Sachs
Macquarie University, Australia

Editorial Board

Professional Learning and Development in Schools and Higher Education disseminates original, research informed writing on the connections between teacher learning and professionalism in schools and higher education. Global in their coverage, the texts deal with the problems and practices of the field in different national and international cultural, policy and practice contexts. The methodology employed encompasses a broad spectrum of conceptual, theoretical, philosophical and empirical research activities. The series explicitly encompasses both the fields of schools and higher education.

The subject areas covered by the series are: professional learning in schools; contexts for professional learning; professional learning in higher education; change; the (new) meanings of professionalism in schools and higher education; training and development in schools and higher education; the 'well-being' agenda in schools and higher education; autonomy, compliance and effectiveness in schools and higher education; principal leadership in schools and higher education; middle-level leadership in schools and higher education.

For other titles published in this series, go to
www.springer.com/series/7908

Lorna M. Earl • Helen Timperley

Editors

Professional Learning Conversations: Challenges in Using Evidence for Improvement

 Springer

Lorna M. Earl
Aporia Consulting Ltd.
Toronto
Canada

Helen Timperley
University of Auckland
Auckland
New Zealand

ISBN: 978-90-481-2356-8 (PB)
ISBN: 978-1-4020-6916-1 (HB)
e-ISBN: 978-1-4020-6917-8

Library of Congress Control Number: 2009922354

Printed on acid-free paper.

9 8 7 6 5 4 3 2 1

springer.com

Acknowledgements

This book has emerged from a long process of discussions among the authors across several continents – by telephone, e-mail and face-to-face, as we grappled with the difficulty of capturing and understanding the way that data are used in education – by teachers, school leaders, policymakers and even students. As editors, we began with the feeling that we had a good idea that deserved attention. As the chapters began to appear from the authors we became even more certain that it is essential to "listen in" to original conversation. Relying on post hoc accounts that were already distilled by the participants could never have provided the detail or the integrity of the thinking and processing that was evident in the original conversations. For this reason, we are deeply indebted to the people in many countries and jurisdictions who allowed the authors to eavesdrop on their interactions with one another. Without their willingness to allow us in, the book would be a shadow of what it has become.

We also want to thank the authors themselves. They have each provided a quality chapter for the work based on their thoughtful and interesting research. When these chapters are taken together, they provide insights that are much deeper than each one on its own. We hope that we have done justice to their contributions in our analysis.

Series Editors Introduction

This, the first book in the series, 'Professional Learning and Development in Schools and Higher Education', is edited by two experienced, committed and skilled educationists from different parts of the world but with converging values and viewpoints. The result is a rich mélange of authors from the USA, Australia, South Africa, Canada and New Zealand all of whom focus on the use of evidence informed decision-making in schools and classrooms. This focus makes for an unusual collection which acts as an antidote to change agendas which are entirely results driven. The book provides evidence from a variety of countries of how system leaders, teachers in schools and higher education must now manage as part of their endeavours to provide the best possible learning and achievement opportunities for all students. What makes this book unique is its engagement with the realities of the challenge of evidence informed conversations which all too quickly become 'activity traps' as teachers are steered away from evidence towards adopting short term pragmatic or ideological solutions which suit the policy agendas of reformists from outside schools and, more often than not, fail to result in real changes in teaching and learning. The editors argue, that, 'having evidence and engaging in conversations will not, by themselves, improve schooling; but that, with the right kind of teacher and school leadership which enables a considered and sustained culture of inquiry, the merging of the process of deep collaboration with evidence and inquiry can create the conditions for generating new knowledge'. This theme of capacity building for change is visited by each of the book's authors. Each story that they tell, each case they analyse, illustrate not only the importance of evidence informed conversations, but, within these, the need to acknowledge their human relationships which are characterized by mutual respect and trust are key to conversations about data which hold possibilities for change. Finally, the collection of papers indicates that systems thoughout the world are engaging with similar issues but there are a variety of strategies that are used to respond to these external pressures. Practitioners and policy makers alike can learn a great deal from the insights presented in this book.

Christopher Day
Judyth Sachs
Series Editors

Contents

Contributors

Editors

Lorna M. Earl is Director, Aporia Consulting, and a recently retired Associate Professor in the Theory and Policy Studies Department and Head of the International Centre for Educational Change at OISE/UT. She was the first Director of Assessment of the Educational Quality and Accountability Office in Ontario and the first Researcher in Residence appointed to the Ontario Ministry of Education. The bulk of her career, however, was spent as a Research Officer and Research Director in several large school districts in Ontario. She has published widely in the areas of assessment, evaluation, and educational change. In recent years she has been involved in writing, research, consultation evaluation, and staff development with teachers' organizations, ministries of education, school boards, and charitable foundations in Canada, England, Australia, New Zealand, Europe and the USA.

Helen Timperley is Professor of Education at the University of Auckland in New Zealand. Her early career involved teaching in early childhood, primary, and secondary education sectors which formed the basis of a research career focused on making a difference to the students this system serves. A particular research emphasis has been on promoting leadership, organizational and professional learning in ways that improve the educational experience of students currently underserved by our education systems. She has recently completed a best-evidence synthesis iteration on professional learning and development, and has published widely in international academic journals such as *Review of Educational Research, Journal of Educational Change, Leadership and Policy in Schools,* and *Journal of Curriculum Studies.* She has written four books in her specialty areas.

Authors

Marnie Curry is a Visiting Professor at Mills College and she also directs Project IMPACT (Inquiry Making Progress Across Communities of Teachers), an induction program based at the University of California, Berkeley. She pursues research on teachers' work lives and focuses on issues related to teachers' professional development, career engagement, and participation in educational reform.

Brahm Fleisch is as an Associate Professor in the Division of Educational Leadership and Policy Studies in the Wits School of Education in Johannesburg, South Africa. He completed his Ph.D. at Columbia University in New York. Since his return to South Africa in 1990, he has lectured at the University of the Witwatersrand, served as a district director in the provincial government, and consulted on education finance, planning, and policy in various countries in Africa. His teaching and research interests include school participation, school effectiveness/improvement, educational finance, education and the law, and educational change. His 2002 book Managing Educational Change: The State and School Reform in South Africa (Heinemann, 2002) provides a comprehensive account of the educational transformation in South African since 1994. His recent publications include the soon to be released Primary Education in Crisis: Why South African Schoolchildren Underachieve in Reading and Mathematics (Juta Press).

Judy Halbert is a co-leader of the Network of Performance Based Schools and an assistant professor in Educational Leadership at the University of Victoria. She has been formally recognized for her excellence in school, provincial and national level leadership. Judy is highly successful in developing strong learning communities through inquiry, thoughtful use of evidence, and teamwork across roles and districts. She is especially interested in the role that formative assessment can play in developing learner confidence and metacognition. The focus of her doctoral study was developing induction programs designed to meet the needs of new principals. Her work in the Certificate of School Management and Leadership program and with leadership development across British Columbia is making a significant difference to the learning lives of young people.

Timothy L. Hopkins is Executive Director of Elementary Education for the Kershaw County School District. His current responsibilities include supervising 11 elementary schools with direct responsibility for ensuring the academic achievement of more than 4,600 students. His previous experiences include school counselor, teacher, principal, and Director of Assessment. A native of Winnsboro, South Carolina, he currently resides in Lugoff, South Carolina. He earned his bachelor's, master's, and education specialist degrees from Winthrop University, Rock Hill, South Carolina.

Linda Kaser is a co-leader of the Network of Performance-Based Schools and an Assistant Professor in Educational Leadership at the University of Victoria. Her doctoral study focused on building trusting relationships with learners, teachers, and families. The application of the findings from her study has made a significant difference to learning at all levels by young people, adults, and families. She is deeply interested in learning more from the aboriginal perspectives in our province, country, and globally. She is recognized provincially and nationally for her work in developing networks that sustain learning change, her interest and application of critical thinking strategies, and her contributions to strengthening the literacy and leadership programs of the province.

Mei Kuin Lai is Associate Director of the Woolf Fisher Research Centre at the University of Auckland. The Centre has a national and international reputation for excellence in research on teaching, learning and development in culturally and linguistically diverse communities. She has research and teaching interests in schooling improvement, in particular research–practice collaborations that improve teaching and learning, and research methodology, and has published work in these areas. Her recent book on practitioner research (Practitioner Research for Educators: A Guide to Improving Classrooms and Schools – Corwin Press 2006) develops theory about, and provides examples of how to conduct, practitioner research for school and classroom improvement. Her current research focus is on sustainability of professional learning and the properties of interventions that raise achievement for linguistically and culturally diverse communities. Since graduating in 2003, Mei has worked in Schooling Improving Initiatives in New Zealand as a researcher-developer and has been in charge of the training program for education consultants (School Support Services Facilitators) at the Faculty of Education to develop inquiry as part of their roles.

Sue Lasky is an Assistant Professor in the College of Education and Human Development at the University of Louisville. Her areas of focus are in policy, and investigating systemic linkages for improvement in culturally and linguistically diverse schools. She has worked in evaluation at the Ontario Institute for Studies in Education at the University of Toronto, where she earned her doctorate, and at the Center for Social Organization of Schools at Johns Hopkins University. She is the sole author of two peer-reviewed articles, coauthor of several book chapters, journal articles, and a book that focused on linkages across the education policy system that can support improved classroom teaching and student learning outcomes.

Linda E. Lee is a partner in Proactive Information Services, a Canadian social research and evaluation company. She has worked in research and evaluation since the late 1970s. She has conducted training on program evaluation, research methods, data use, student assessment, organizational change, and education for social justice. She has worked extensively in the area of school improvement, including workshops in Canada, Europe, and South America. She is passionate about using evidence, empowering students, and engaging school communities in improving educational equity and access, all with the intention of creating a more socially just world.

Judith Warren Little is Professor of Education at the Graduate School of Education, University of California, Berkeley. Her research focuses on teachers' work and on the organizational and policy contexts of teaching and teacher learning. She concentrates especially on the nature of teachers' professional community and its relationship to teacher development and school reform, investigating how teachers' interactions with one another in ordinary workplace settings and in formal professional development contexts supply resources for teacher learning and the improvement of practice.

Stuart McNaughton is Professor of Education at the University of Auckland and Director of the Woolf Fisher Research Centre. The Centre has a national and international reputation for excellence in research on teaching, learning, and development in culturally and linguistically diverse communities. He has research and teaching interests in developmental and educational psychology with a focus on the development of language and literacy, and processes of education, socialization, and culture. Publications include books on reading and instruction (Being Skilled: The Socialisation of Learning to Read – Methuen 1987) and emergent literacy (Patterns of Emergent Literacy: Processes of Development and Transition – Oxford University Press, 1995), and papers and presentations on many aspects of teaching, learning, and development in family and school settings. His most recent book (Meeting of Minds – Learning Media 2002) develops a theory about, and gives extensive examples of, effective literacy instruction for culturally and linguistically diverse children.

Eugene C. Schaffer is a Professor of Education at the University of Maryland, Baltimore County. He has served as Chair of the Department of Education at the University of Maryland Baltimore County, and Chair of Curriculum and Instruction at the University of North Carolina Charlotte. His current research includes an experimental study of at-risk schools and the development of highly reliable schools. He has coauthored two books, a monograph, six book chapters and over 30 refereed journal articles as well as numerous research reports and conference papers. A Fulbright recipient to Taiwan and the Republic of Slovakia, he served as member of the faculties at Valparaiso University, University of North Carolina Charlotte, National Kaohsiung Normal University (Taiwan), and Tokyo University.

Chapter 1
Understanding How Evidence and Learning Conversations Work

Lorna M. Earl and Helen Timperley

Introduction

The experiences of the last 25 years have shown us that changing schools in any large-scale and sustainable way is a difficult and challenging process (Elmore, 1996). Jurisdictions around the world are struggling to find strategies and processes that will result in enhanced learning for students and receive widespread support in the educational community and beyond.

School leaders are faced with the daunting task of anticipating the future and making conscious adaptations to their practices, in order to keep up and be responsive to an ever-changing environment. To succeed in a rapidly changing and increasingly complex world, it is vital that schools grow, develop, adapt and take charge of change so that they can control their own futures (Stoll, Fink and Earl, 2003). Schools that are able to take charge of change, rather than being controlled by it, have been shown to be more effective and improve more rapidly than ones that are not (Rosenholz, 1989; Stoll and Fink, 1996; Gray et al., 1999).

Like many others in the knowledge society, the educational community has become aware that having and using knowledge wisely is an essential skill. At all levels from the classroom to the school, from the district to the central authority, they are increasingly drawing on evidence, data and information and providing substantiation for the decisions that they make. Most jurisdictions engage in a range of processes to provide evidence for their decision-making and use large-scale assessment systems, surveys, research studies and existing literature to provide evidence that can inform their thinking and their decisions in such diverse areas as policy discussions, school planning, and classroom practice.

This book emerged from our interest in seeing how evidence is being introduced and used in education and, more particularly, understanding how educators at all levels actually use evidence in their thinking and their decision-making. Our work over the last decade, across several continents, has focused on how educational practitioners, leaders and policymakers refer to and use evidence in their decision-making. In particular, we have both been engaged in a number of projects that examine the way individuals and groups of people approach, engage with, interpret and use a range of data sources in making educational decisions (Earl and Katz,

L.M. Earl and H. Timperley (eds.), *Professional Learning Conversations:*
Challenges in Using Evidence for Improvement.
© Springer Science+Business Media B.V. 2009

2006; Timperley, 2005a, 2005b, 2006). This work, and the work of others (Argyris and Schön, 1996; Phillips, 2003; Robinson and Walker, 1999), has led us to believe that conversations that are grounded in evidence and focused on learning from that evidence have considerable potential to influence what happens in schools and ultimately enhance the quality and the efficiency of student learning. We have also come to the conclusion that having conversations based on data in educational contexts is very hard to do. It is hard because productive use of evidence requires more than just adding data to the conversation; it involves a way of thinking and challenging ideas towards new knowledge.

As we have engaged with decision-makers concerned with policy, leadership and classroom practice, we have been struck by the frequency with which people use data to begin a discussion but quickly move to solutions that are not well founded in the evidence at hand. This is a phenomenon that has been described by Katz, Earl and Ben Jaafar (forthcoming) as "activity traps" – moving quickly to doing, to being busy and to feeling productive, without sufficient attention to selecting the right things to do in the circumstances.

In this volume, we explore how conversations structured to make sense of various forms of evidence can result in real changes in student learning. Our broader theory of action is straightforward, but complex. It is based on the intersection of theory about epistemology, inquiry and social construction of learning and is premised on the conviction that significant change in schooling depends on the creation of new knowledge for the adults who are making the decisions. This new knowledge will change the kinds of policies that are set, how leaders work in districts and schools, how teachers engage with students in their classrooms and how students interact with one another.

Although this book is about having conversations based on evidence, having evidence and engaging in conversations will not, by themselves, improve schooling. Instead, the merging of the process of deep collaboration with evidence and inquiry can create the conditions for generating new knowledge. As Hakkarainen, Paavola and Lehtinen (2004) describe, knowledge is created through dialogue or conversations that make presuppositions, ideas, beliefs and feelings explicit and available for exploration. It is in these conversations that new ideas, tools and practices are created, and the initial knowledge is either substantially enriched or transformed during the process. Innovative solutions arise when people in groups draw on evidence and on outside explicit knowledge and combine it with tacit knowledge in response to authentic problems (Nonaka and Takeuchi, 1995). It is our contention that when educators engage in conversations about what evidence means, it sets the stage for new knowledge to emerge as the participants encounter new ideas or discover that ideas that they have held as "truth" do not hold up under scrutiny and they use the recognition as an opportunity to rethink what they know and what they do.

The engagement of competing theories and the evidence underpinning them requires the participants in a conversation to reveal what they believe and why. They must explain their views and why their perspective is preferable to those of others, and also be open to challenge and critique. Often personal theories about "what" are implicit rather than explicit and assumed rather than tested. Through the process of explaining these theories to others who hold different views, what is known is made more explicit together with the values, beliefs and evidence that underpin them.

In the next section, we ground our theory of action in a theoretical model that describes what we believe are the qualities of productive evidence-informed conversations, to show both why we think that productive conversations about evidence can change practices and ultimately student learning and also why we think these conversations are (and will be) hard work.

Qualities of Productive Evidence-informed Conversations

It should be clear that our conception of productive evidence-informed conversation is not formulaic and it includes more than conversations with some attention to evidence. Instead, it is an iterative process of asking questions, examining evidence and thinking about what the evidence means in the particular context (see Earl and Katz, 2006[1]). We believe that the qualities that are required in these kinds of conversations are having an "inquiry habit of mind", considering a broad range of "relevant evidence" and engaging in "learning conversations". We argue that, taken together, these three qualities provide the basis for evidence-informed educational improvement. None of them, on their own, is sufficient, however, and the absence of any one of them can lead to serious misinterpretations and bad decisions.

Figure 1.1 illustrates how the three qualities we have outlined above, an inquiry habit of mind, the nature of evidence informing our theories, and learning conversations

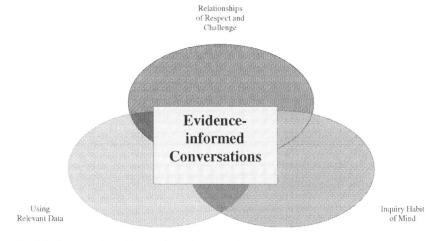

Fig. 1.1 Processes for evidence-informed conversations

---

[1] Many of the ideas included in this chapter have emerged from work on using data that one of us (Earl) has done with Steven Katz. We are indebted to him for his contribution to our thinking.

interact to make for a powerful collaborative inquiry improvement process. It will be clear from the discussion that follows that these processes are intimately inter-linked and, from our view, are all necessary to move towards genuine and continual improvements in schooling.

Inquiry Habit of Mind

The notion of an inquiry habit of mind refers to an ongoing process of using evidence to make decisions. Inquiry is, very simply, a way of finding things out – collecting data and interpreting evidence in ways that enhance and advance understanding. The *Oxford English Dictionary* (Allen, 1991) defines a habit as:

> a settled or tendency of practice; practice that is hard to give up; mental constitution.

This notion effectively describes what we are holding out as an organizational "way of being". Habits of mind incorporate dispositional, emotional, motivational and personality variables that contribute to competence in managing the environment and making decisions (Keating, 1996). We link inquiry to habit of mind to emphasize that this is a way of thinking that is a dynamic system of feedback loops that moves towards clearer directions and decisions and draws on, or seeks out, information as the participants become closer to understanding some phenomenon. Having an inquiry habit of mind is premised on a recognition that all decision-making includes a certain amount of guessing, and that it is possible to use a range of evidence to both shape and limit the guesswork involved.

Operating with an inquiry habit of mind is not a typical approach for many peo-ple. What people know very much depends on how they come to know it. Each person creates their own knowledge and understanding throughout their lives by connecting what is being learned with prior knowledge and experience (Lambert and McCombs, 1998). We are all products of our personal histories, training and experiences at schools, and engage in educational decision-making in ways that are consistent with our personal knowledge and our implicit theories about learning, about students and about schools. These views may arise from our experiences at school (as students and as teachers) or from the prevailing ideologies within the society at the time.

How people acquire knowledge proves that there are inevitable differences in what is accepted as knowledge and as best practice. These differences can create misunderstanding, inefficiencies and, sometimes, even conflict about schooling. The world that individuals construct for themselves includes their beliefs about how important values and goals can be achieved under particular conditions or circum-stances (Robinson and Walker, 1999). This personal theory is coherent and makes sense within their personal frame of reference and provides the framework for the interpretation of new information (Lipman, 1991; Reynolds, Sinatra and Jetton, 1996). Unless something happens to challenge these ideas, such as new or discrepant ideas, there is no need to move beyond them.

One of the central premises of this book is that it is necessary to approach decision-making with an inquiry habit of mind (Earl and Katz, 2006) and a belief that improvements occur through engaging with the ideas of others and the evidence on which these ideas are based. Rather than viewing differences as problematic, they need to be viewed as having the potential to increase the quality of ideas and information that can be brought to improving practice. Differences between theories about the current situation and how to improve it are expected and accepted. If the theories and their explanations are restricted to personal values and beliefs, however, the discussion may result in mutual understanding and a sense of goodwill, but they may still reflect individual impressions. To achieve deeper understanding about an issue, the agreement must be based on evidence that can be examined and tested.

Because the way in which evidence is interpreted is strongly influenced by the theories we bring to the exercise, there are as likely to be as many differences in interpretation as there are theories. Skills in interpretation and experience with different forms of evidence also influence what conclusions are drawn. Although we will address skill-related issues in a subsequent section of this chapter, we suggest that the disposition to be open to a range of interpretations is probably more important. It is to this attribute we turn next.

An inquiry habit of mind presupposes a mind-set of being in charge of one's personal destiny and creating or locating the knowledge that will be useful along the way. As Senge (1990) said, a learning organization is one that is "continually expanding its capacity to create its future". It is not a linear or mechanistic process, but an iterative process of "thinking in circles" (O'Connor and McDermott, 1997) with a series of decisions, actions and feedback loops guiding the process. They need to want to know, even when the knowing is difficult or contrary to their beliefs. Leaders with an inquiry habit of mind do not presume an outcome; instead they allow for a range of outcomes and keep searching for increased understanding and clarity. Inquiry-mindedness demands engagement in questioning, reflecting and decision-making, using data as a critical element in the process. What does this mean for educators?

Valuing Deep Understanding

Educators, whether leaders or teachers, make hundreds of decisions in a day. Not every decision requires a major research study. However, decisions that have far-reaching consequences or are high stakes deserve to be investigated thoroughly through the lenses of pertinent data, as a way of either validating hunches or rethinking ideas. All too often, educators use data to support narrow or parochial causes – to fight turf wars, impede change or justify decisions that have already been made (Knight Higher Education Collaborative, 2000). It is human nature to look for confirmatory evidence. It is harder but more useful to look beyond the obvious to make sense of something. The first step in being inquiry-minded is captured in the Platonic notion aporia – recognizing that you do not know and being determined to get increasing clarity and understanding.

Reserving Judgment and Having a Tolerance for Ambiguity

It is all too easy to find information that confirms one's biases and look no further. The inquiry-minded leader eschews such false closure and refuses to accept the first or, indeed, any interpretations or decisions that are hasty or unsubstantiated, no matter how appealing. Education in the 21st century is full of uncertainty, surprises and rapid change. Ambiguity is an inevitable part of social systems that are in constant motion. Inquiry-mindedness requires a tolerance for this uncertainty and a willingness to live in the dissonance long enough to investigate and explore ideas through the lenses of evidence until there is some clarity about what it might mean. Having an inquiry habit of mind means thinking through and working with the ideas, even when solutions seem illusive. When the solutions are murky, it is likely that more information is needed, and that means more time and more thinking, as well.

Taking a Range of Perspectives and Posing Increasingly Focused Questions

In complex environments answers are rarely obvious or straightforward. Instead, considering the issues carefully usually leads to more and more focused investigation and to better questions. If clarity is the end, then thinking from multiple perspectives is the means. Leaders need to stand back and view the situation through a myriad of lenses and to narrow the investigation.

The next link in the chain between engagement and achievement is more difficult to establish. One of the difficulties in determining whether increased engagement impacts on achievement is the time lag between these two events, and so may require longer-term monitoring.

Using Relevant Data

Generally educators find local, anecdotal knowledge more powerful than knowledge developed through research because it is more personal and is perceived to relate directly to the context in which improvement is sought. Experienced educators, whatever their role, build up rich personal encyclopedias of situations and appropriate actions that allow them to become experts in their fields of operation. Although this knowledge base is sufficient for many situations, it is often based on assumptions about outcomes, rather than being subjected to any real test of those assumptions. Western education systems have a history of being driven by "inputs" – "If x happens, then y will surely follow." Often x takes the form of resources or particular forms of professional development. Unfortunately, despite the inputs of increasing resources and opportunities for professional development, the desired outcomes have not necessarily followed, particularly in relation to some entrenched problems in education, such as the achievement of traditionally disengaged and underachieving student populations (Elmore, 1996).

Whatever form of evidence is used to test whether desired outcomes have been achieved, it rarely speaks for itself. Most evidence, whether based on personal observations or test results, can be interpreted in many different ways and is as likely to be as contested as the theories on which it is based. In our middle school example, improvements in test scores may be declared statistically significant by researchers, for example, but fail the test of "educational" significance by those on the ground because the gains are so small. Alternatively, the teachers may see that some individuals have become much more engaged in school through participating in extracurricular activities, but fail the statistician's test of significant improvement in their test scores. There are many different types of evidence in education and many educational dimensions that are important for educators to consider when they are making decisions about practices. We contend that evidence can be very far-reaching and provide insights into such things as beliefs, convictions, behaviors and influences on practice. It can represent intangible concepts like intelligence or learning or community perceptions. It can come in the form of statistical summaries, or testimonials or incident reports. However construed, evidence can be independently observed and verified and there is broad consensus as to its contents, even if its interpretation is contested. The value and utility associated with evidence comes from the care with which the information has been collected and collated and from transforming it into knowledge by shaping it, organizing it and thinking about what it might mean.

Using evidence for planning and decision-making does require that educators develop some new skills, especially in relation to the statistical information that constitutes one kind of data source. As one of us has written elsewhere, building on a concept put forward by Stiggins (1995):

> We live in a culture that has come to value and depend on statistical information to inform our decisions. At the same time, we are likely to misunderstand and misuse those statistics because we are "statistically illiterate" and consequently have no idea what the numbers mean. (Earl, 1995, p. 27)

Not much has changed since that time. One of the most distressing findings in our evaluation of the National Literacy and Numeracy Strategies in England (one of the most data-rich countries in the world) was the variability in people's knowledge of what the various forms of evidence mean and how such information might contribute to decisions. In some places, data were viewed as important tools to focus discussion and challenge opinions. When in doubt, the participants looked for additional information to clarify their thinking. In other cases, however, the data were seen as absolute and inviolate and the interpretation was often superficial and viewed as unequivocal (Earl, Levin, Leithwood, Fullan and Watson, 2001).

If educators are going to be active in interpreting and using data, as well as challenging and disputing interpretations or uses that they believe are contestable, they must become knowledgeable about judging the value and quality of the evidence and thinking and talking about its meaning. They need clarity of purpose, criteria to judge the quality of the evidence, knowledge about statistical and measurement concepts, and, most importantly, they need to make interpretation paramount (Earl and Katz, 2006).

Clarifying Purpose(s)

When educators are clear about their purposes, they search out the evidence that will provide them with deeper understanding. All too often educational decisions are made using data that are available, rather than data that are appropriate. Different purposes suggest a need for different evidence, based on the questions to be answered and the phenomenon to be understood.

Recognizing Sound and Unsound Evidence

Evidence, whether numerical (e.g., test scores or performance indicators) or narrative (e.g., interviews or testimonials), is made up of symbolic representations of some underlying ideas. They are estimates, with some degree of uncertainty, not absolute measurements. The information has been collected by someone, analyzed by someone and summarized by someone. None of these activities is infallible, whether they involve statistics or stories.

One of the first challenges for anyone who is using evidence is to ascertain the quality of the evidence that they intend to use. There are many examples of inaccurate or misleading evidence contributing to bad decisions. Leaders must be able to discern between legitimate evidence and evidence that is suspect.

Having Knowledge About Statistical and Measurement Concepts

Data in education are generally measurements of something, often analyzed using statistics. But statistics strike fear into the hearts of many people. For the most part, educators have not seen statistics as a useful addition to their tool kit for decision-making. Instead, statistics are either imbued with a magical quality of numerical "truth", or they are mistrusted as blatant attempts to distort or manipulate an audience. Neither of these positions is defensible. Like a meterstick, statistics are tools designed to provide accurate and consistent measurements. Unlike a meterstick, they are not used to measure something that is visible and can be checked easily. Human characteristics, like learning and achievement are much more difficult to measure than physical objects. Tests and statistical procedures have been developed to try to provide **estimates** of these invisible human qualities. There are conventions and rules for the measurement of student achievement that are extremely important, especially when the results are being used to make significant decisions.

Using data requires familiarity with the language of statistics. If leaders are going to use data to enhance rather than distort educational decisions, they have a responsibility to understand the principles that underlie the statistics in order to be able to distinguish honest, useful conclusions from skulduggery or foolishness (Abelson, 1995).

Making Interpretation Paramount

Evidence of all sorts provides the tools for measuring important educational concepts, but the evidence is only as good as the thinking that goes into the interpretation. Evidence does not provide right answers or quick fixes. Instead, it provides the substance for the conversations that ensue. Fullan (2001) expresses it simply as "the problem of meaning is central to making sense of educational change". Evidence, presented in a variety of ways, offers an opportunity to view a phenomenon through a number of different lenses, to put forward hypotheses, to challenge beliefs and to pose more questions. Interpretation requires time, thoughtfulness, reservation of judgments and open challenge of, as well as support for, ideas. Very often, it also requires more information along the way to clarify or extend the possibilities. Interpretation, then, is thinking – formulating possibilities, developing convincing arguments, locating logical flaws and establishing a feasible and defensible notion of what the data represent.

Conversations are central to these interpretation processes. While many of us experience fear when faced with statistics, most of us believe we know how to have a conversation. Yet the research in this area by Argyris and Schön (1996) tells us that having the types of conversations that incorporate the qualities identified above is extremely challenging. These challenges involve new skills but most importantly they involve redefining what it means for the kinds of conversations we have with our colleagues.

Relationships of Respect and Challenge

Throughout this introductory chapter we have implied, but not made explicit, that the context for determining improvement is social rather than individual. While individual reflection can be a powerful process for identifying issues and the processes for improvement, if those reflections remain with the individual, patches of brilliance may result, but these patches are unlikely to become institutionalized beyond an individual teacher's classroom or administrator's responsibilities. If knowledge is to become more generic, it needs to be socially constructed by the key participants, the merits debated and the potential flaws exposed. Dialogue typically forms the medium through which this social construction takes place.

Argyris and Schön (1996) identify that conversations which promote the learning of all participants in ways that develop enduring solutions include the attributes we have identified above. There is one more attribute, however, that we have not mentioned specifically and this involves understanding what it means to show mutual respect in such conversations. Showing respect is often interpreted as giving equal airtime to the ideas and opinions of all those participating in a conversation and accepting different accounts as equally valid (Timperley, 2005). Showing respect in this way, however, is typically not effective in improving teaching or leadership practice. Improvement does involve showing respect by taking the time to understand each others' viewpoints because there are always many sides to a story, but the purpose is to probe meanings, challenge each others' interpretations of the evidence and the reasoning on which the different viewpoints are based. Respect, therefore, is as much about challenge as it is about support, with a key value being respect for the capacity of all involved to learn and improve.

The framework we are proposing for such dialogue or conversations is "learning conversations" (Robinson; 1993; Timperley, 2001) because they encompass many of the qualities of the ideas expressed above. The basis of learning conversations is the mutual understanding of each contributor's claims and the values, together with the reasoning and data on which they are based. These processes relate to each aspect of improving practice, whether identifying the current situation and its merits and difficulties, deciding the goals of improvement, or how best to get there.

Witnessing Evidence-informed Learning Conversations

Our purpose in this book is to allow the reader to "listen in" on snippets of conversations based on evidence at all levels of the educational system. In each of the chapters, the authors give excerpts of real conversations that they were privileged to witness and to capture. They occur at many levels of the education system, from policymakers, schooling improvement coordinators, leaders, teachers and students. They take place across the globe including the USA, Canada, New Zealand and South Africa. They include a variety of evidence encompassing students' test results as well as examining the quality of student work.

The authors of the chapters that follow have used conversations to examine and highlight possibilities and pitfalls of engaging in conversations grounded in evidence as mechanisms to improve educational outcomes. The conversations themselves have been selected to provide rich images of how evidence-informed conversations work (or do not work) and to exemplify some of the principles of knowledge creation at work. For the most part, the conversations were longer than the authors' presence and, in some cases, they extended over several months as the group revisited the same issues more than once.

This variety of contexts shows some unifying themes and key challenges. Regardless of where the conversations take place or who the participants are, it is readily apparent that they are difficult to have in ways that get to the heart of issues identified in the evidence and lead to improvements in practice. The extremes of success and failure included in these chapters could lead to some thought-provoking insights. Chapter 5 by Linda Kaser and Judy Halbert, for example, analyzes a conversation between students that clearly leads to learning and improvement. In contrast, Chapter 9 by Brahm Fleisch illustrates how conflicting agendas and politics intrude on the conversations among policymakers, leading to escalating attributions of blame and the entrenchment of predetermined positions. It is just possible that the policymakers might learn from listening into the students' conversations.

Another common theme throughout the chapters is the very steep learning curve involved in moving from producing and examining data to using it for improvement purposes. Most chapters show an international trend towards producing data – masses of it. They also illustrate the difficulties evident across the globe in interpreting and using those data for the purposes of school improvement. Some do so much more successfully than others. Our opening chapter by Mei Kuin Lai and Stuart McNaughton (Chapter 2) illustrates the most developed use of evidence for improvement at a systems and school level. These conversations were able to take place only after years of training and involvement in moving from evidence to meaningful and targeted action based on the analysis of multiple and sometimes conflicting data sources. The chapter may, however, provide some inspiration and guidance for those struggling to have such conversations. Judith Warren Little and Marnie Currie (Chapter 3), on the other hand, show how difficult it is for a group to move beyond superficial conversations and avoid issues of professional expertise, even after considerable training and experience with protocols to guide them.

The final theme we will highlight in this introductory section is how leadership has emerged as a key theme in the different chapters. How leaders bridge the interaction between the data and the participants in the conversations makes the difference. Leaders are instrumental in developing the norms of trust and respect essential to successful conversations. At the same time, they need the skills and courage to remain focused on the learning challenges and to insist that it is the action following from the data that makes the difference. This theme is investigated in the chapters by Earl and Timperley (Chapters 4, 6 and 10).

References

Abelson, R. (1995). *Statistics as principled argument*. Hillsdale, NJ: Lawerence Erlbaum Associates.

Allen, R. E. (Ed.). (1991). *Oxford English dictionary*. New York: Oxford University Press.

Argyris, C., & Schön, D. (1996). *Organizational learning II*. Reading, MA.: Addison-Wesley.

Earl, L. (1995). Moving from the political to the practical: A hard look at assessment and accountability. Orbit, Toronto: Ontario Institute for Education. Vol. 26(2).

Earl, L., & Katz, S. (2006). *Leading in a data rich world*. Thousand Oaks, CA: Corwin Press.

Earl, L., Levin, B., Leithwood, K., Fullan, M., & Watson, N. (2001). *Watching and learning 2: OISE/UT Evaluation of the implementation of the national literacy and numeracy strategies in England*. London: Department for Education and Employment.

Elmore, R. F. (1996). Getting to scale with good educational practice. *Harvard Educational Review*, *66*(1), 1–26.

Fullan, M. (2001). *The meaning of educational change* (3rd ed.). New York: Teachers' College Press.

Gray, J., Hopkins, D., Reynolds, D., Wilcox, B., Farrel, S., & Jesson, D. (1999). *Improving schools: Performance and potential*. Buckingham, UK: Open University Press.

Hakkarainen, T., Paavola, S., & Lehtinen, E. (2004). *Communites of networked expertise: Professional and educational perspectives*. Amsterdam: Elsevier.

Katz, S., Earl, L., & Ben Jaafar, S. (2006). *Networking schools for learning*. Thousand Oaks, CA: Corwin Press.

Keating, D. (1996). Habits of mind for a learning society: Educating for human development. In D. Olson & N. Torrance (Eds.), *The Handbook of education and human development* (pp. 461–481). Cambridge, MA: Blackwell.

Knight Higher Education Collaborative (2000). The data made me do it. *Policy Perspectives*, *9*(2), 1–12.

Lambert, N., & McCombs, B. (1998). *How students learn: Reforming schools through learner-centered education*. Washington, DC: APA.

Lipman, M. (1991). *Thinking in education*. Cambridge: Cambridge University Press.

Nonaka, I., & Takeuchi, H. (1995). *The knowledge-creating company*. Oxford: Oxford University Press.

O'Connor, J., & McDermott, I. (1997). *The art of systems thinking*. London: Thorsons.

Phillips, J. (2003). Powerful learning: Creating learning communities in urban school reform. *Journal of Curriculum and Supervision*, *18*(3), 240–258.

Reynolds, R., Sinatra, G., & Jetton, T. (1996). Views of knowledge acquisition and representation: A continuum from experience centered to mind centered. *Educational Psychology*, *31*(2), 93–104.

Robinson, V., & Walker, J. (1999). Theoretical privilege and researchers' contribution to educational change. In J. S. Gaffney & B. J. Askew (Eds.), *Stirring the waters: The influence of Marie Clay* (pp. 349–381). Portsmouth, NH: Heinemann.

Robinson, V. M. J. (1993). *Problem-based methodology: Research for the improvement of practice*. Oxford: Pergamon Press.

Rosenholz, S. (1989). *Teachers' workplace*. New York: Teachers College Press.

Senge, P. (1990). *The fifth discipline: The art and practice of the learning organization*. London: Random House.

Stiggins, R. (1995). Assessment literacy for the 21st century. *Phi Delta Kappan*, November, 238–245.

Stoll, L., & Fink, D. (1996). *Changing our schools*. Philadelphia, PA: Open University Press.

Stoll, L., Fink, D., & Earl, L. (2003). *It's about learning: And it's about time*. London: Falmer Routledge.

Timperley, H. S. (2001). Mentoring conversations designed to promote student teacher learning. *Asia-Pacific Journal of Teacher Education*, *29*(2), 111–123.

Timperley, H. S. (2005). Distributed leadership: Developing theory from practice. *Journal of Curriculum Studies*, *37*(6), 395–420.

Timperley, H. S. (2005a). Distributed leadership: Developing theory from practice. *Journal of Curriculum Studies*, *37*(6), 395–420.

Timperley, H. S. (2005b). Instructional leadership challenges: The case of using student achievement information for instructional improvement. *Leadership and Policy in Schools*, *4*(1), 3–22.

Timperley, H. S. (2006). Learning challenges involved in developing leading for learning. *Educational Management Administration and Leadership*, *34*(4), 549–566.

Chapter 2
Raising Student Achievement in Poor Communities Through Evidence-Based Conversations

Mei Kuin Lai and Stuart McNaughton

Chapter Overview *Improving the academic achievement of traditionally underserved students in New Zealand provided the context for this chapter by* **Mei Kuin Lai** *and* **Stuart McNaughton**. *In their conversations as researchers with a network of school leaders and teachers, these authors show how prior training in interpreting and using evidence led to sophisticated interpretations that were effective in providing the basis for improving instructional practice. An iterative process involving developing questions, gathering data to test different theories of identified problems, developing solutions and posing more focused questions were evident in the participants' conversations and actions. The authors propose that the conditions enabling these conversations to occur included a professional community prepared to put their students' needs above their own comfort by raising difficult issues, and sufficient knowledge to interpret the data while identifying what more they needed to know.*

Around the world, educators working in poor communities face a common challenge. The challenge is to improve the academic achievement of their students, who in many instances are culturally and linguistically diverse and achieve below national expectations. Research development programs designed to raise achievement focus on a variety of components. In some, educators work with the community to support parents to teach their children; in others, researchers work on large-scale interventions to improve the teaching pedagogy; in still others, private consultants and companies offer programs and resources to address these students' needs. In an environment of multiple choices and little evidence of sustainable improvements (e.g., Annan, 2007; Borman, Hewes, Overman and Brown, 2002), it is important to identify what makes the most difference. This identification helps educators sift out the gold from the dross and do what is best for their students.

It is in this context that we examine the contribution of evidence-informed conversations. By using a case study from a medium-scale intervention serving a poor, suburban community of primarily indigenous and minority ethnic groups in New Zealand, we illustrate how evidence-informed conversations contributed to improving student achievement. In our first example, we demonstrate how such

L.M. Earl and H. Timperley (eds.), *Professional Learning Conversations:*
Challenges in Using Evidence for Improvement.
© Springer Science+Business Media B.V. 2009

conversations with researchers helped teachers and school leaders to identify what to alter in their teaching programs to better meet student needs. The conversations involved interpreting evidence from student assessments and observing teaching to learn how to solve the problems identified through more effective teaching.

In our second example, we show how applying an inquiry habit of mind (one of the three elements in inquiry-based conversations using evidence) helped teachers and school leaders to recognize that they did not need to change an existing practice. Knowing that no alterations to teaching programs are needed is as important as knowing what to alter, particularly for schools with multiple pressing educational needs and an already crowded curriculum. The inquiry process led to the discovery of a new educational problem illustrated in our third example. This example describes the iterative nature of inquiry, of continually seeking evidence and posing increasingly focused questions to understand the nature of the problem, and shows how applying an inquiry habit of mind iteratively to a pressing educational problem supported the educators to increase their understanding of the problem and its complexities.

Context

The context for the conversations was a schooling improvement initiative in New Zealand schools which served poor, suburban communities comprising minority and indigenous students facing high levels of underachievement. The goal of the initiative was to offer high-quality learning environments to raise achievement in those schools.

The intervention described in this chapter was part of this initiative and involved a 3-year research and development collaboration between seven schools and a university-based research center to improve reading comprehension in 9–14-year-olds. Previous assessments collected by the schools using standardized achievement tests showed low levels of reading comprehension. All schools faced the same problem and decided to work together with support from the researchers to improve it. Given the many competing possible approaches, they decided to investigate, rather than assume, what students really needed. Phase one of the intervention involved school leaders and researchers collaborating to examine student achievement in reading comprehension and to observe how teachers taught reading. The aim was to assist teachers to understand students' strengths and weaknesses and to understand how their own classroom practices might be strengthened.

A professional learning community comprising school and Ministry of Education representatives and researchers worked together to examine evidence about the quality of reading instruction and its impact on comprehension. Similar communities of teachers and administrators were formed within each school. These professional learning communities all set specific goals and designed processes to begin rigorous investigations into school-wide teaching and learning.

Two years prior to the intervention described in this chapter, school leaders and teachers underwent training in critically examining data. The training program included, amongst other things, how to collect reliable observations of student reading across schools, how to conduct learning conversations and how to analyze student achievement data (Mose and Annan, 2003). The latter included a mastery task where all school leaders had to demonstrate that they could analyze patterns of student achievement, propose theories about the reasons for the achievement patterns, collect data to check these theories and develop programs to raise achievement. Thus, by the time of the intervention, the school leaders were already focused on what they could do to raise achievement.

The data discussed in these conversations were the findings from two standardized reading assessments of reading comprehension and classroom observations. The student achievement data were analyzed to examine overall achievement in reading comprehension and to identify students' strengths and weaknesses. Observations were analyzed to understand how features of teaching and learning might map on to the achievement data. All these analyses were collaboratively discussed with teachers and school leaders in professional learning communities, as the following examples will illustrate.

Example 1: Discussing the Link Between Student Learning and Teaching Practices

In conducting inquiry-based conversations using evidence, it is important for educators to begin with a clear purpose so they can search out appropriate evidence to provide them with deep understanding as described in the introductory chapter (Chapter 1) to this book. Teachers and school leaders in the professional learning community had two key questions:

- "What are we doing which could have influenced the pattern of student achievement results?"
- "How can we improve what we are doing to raise student achievement?"

In order to answer these questions, teachers and school leaders had to be able to identify (through the analysis of students' tests scores and answers) students' strengths and weaknesses and build a profile of learning needs. They also had to identify and evaluate the effectiveness of their own classroom practice in relation to these needs. The next step, therefore, was to link the various types of evidence collected to better understand how to support students' learning. In this example, we focus on one aspect of the test, paragraph comprehension, which the analysis had uncovered as a weakness through profiling students' learning from the test (Lai, McNaughton, MacDonald and Farry, 2004).The test consisted of four subtests: decoding, sentence comprehension, paragraph comprehension and vocabulary. Paragraph comprehension was assessed through a cloze passage, in which students were required to read a paragraph with some of the words omitted, and find an appropriate replacement for the omitted words. Figure 2.1 compares the four subtests against the national norms for each subtest.

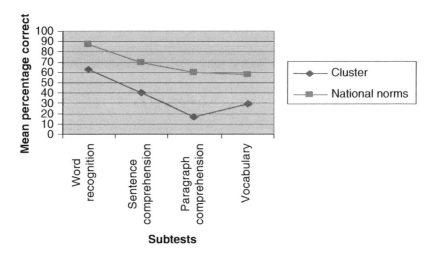

Fig. 2.1 Average subtest score (in percentages) correctly answered for the cluster against national norms (year 4)

The following is an example conversation around this profiling.

Mei: *What does this graph tell you about students' strengths and weaknesses?*
Teacher 4:   *Decoding is their strength. The word recognition subtest is pretty close to national norms.*
Mei: *So what does that mean, educationally that is?*
Teacher 1:   *They can bark at text but can't understand what they are reading.*
Teacher 2:   *Yeah. Look at paragraph comprehension. It is very weak. On average, they are only scoring 20%!*
Teacher 3:   *That is really low. That's about 4 out of 20 isn't it?*
Teacher 2:   *Yes. Their vocabulary is pretty weak too. It might be linked.*
Teacher 4:   *We should look at the other year levels too. Are they all equally weak at paragraph comprehension? Is this a problem across the whole school?*

Students' scores on the paragraph comprehension subtest were well-below national profiles, and in some year levels, below the critical score, which indicated they were having serious difficulties (Elley, 2001; Lai et al., 2004). When the researchers analyzed the test in greater detail, they noticed that students appeared to be overpredicting or guessing in the cloze passages. Their mistakes made sense in the presentence context but resulted in nonsense or illogical sentences. They were not checking their answers. The following are examples of students' responses in italics and the correct response(s) in brackets

All they did (could) afford was a tiny room in a shoe (cottage/house/shop) in a village by a river.
He grabbed frantically and felt his head (hand(s)/finger(s)) closing around the branch of a tree.

The classroom observations showed that checking for textual evidence when comprehending a text occurred only nine times in 16 h of observations (Lai et al., 2004;

McNaughton, MacDonald, Amituanai-Toloa, Lai & Farry 2006. For example, across all classes in all activities, predictions were often prompted for word meanings and event sequences, but all contributions were accepted with phrases such as *Good prediction* and *That was clever*, even if the prediction bore no relationship to the story. Students were not required to check their answers against the information in the text, which could explain why they did not check their answers in the cloze passage in the assessment to see if they made sense.

An inquiry habit of mind requires educators to refuse to accept the first, or indeed any, interpretations that are hasty, no matter how appealing (Earl and Timperley, Chapter 1 this Volume). So, rather than present this link between teachers' prompting students to check for textual evidence and students' patterns of errors as "fact", the researchers raised this as a possible theory to be discussed by the whole professional learning community. The researchers did not see their theory as infallible, but allowed all members of the community to critique their theory (Robinson and Lai, 2006).

When this evidence was presented, school leaders and teachers recognized the need for checking. They started providing their own examples of problems with textual checking when teaching comprehension in their schools. An administrator from one school, for example, commented on what she had observed: "A teacher was reading a story about the beach and asked the students to predict what happened next. The student said, 'They fly to the moon!' " (Robinson and Lai, 2006, p. 203). The teacher did not require the student to check his answer against the information in the story.

So school leaders and teachers agreed with the researchers that the link between these teaching practices and the pattern of achievement was plausible and began to discuss how to incorporate more checking into their programs. The researchers did not explicitly tell the practitioners how to increase checking, but left them to design their own ways of doing so in interschool and intraschool professional learning meetings. One school, for example, came up with their own school-wide program which was an adaptation of a current resource. This resource required students to look at an illustration from a book and make predictions about the story. The adaptation required students to find evidence to support or disconfirm their predictions after reading the story.

Outcomes: When teachers were observed at the beginning of the following year, there was a substantial change in checking for textual evidence when reading. Twenty percent of all exchanges between children and teachers now contained some reference to checking textual evidence by either teacher or child, and occurred about once every 7–8 min. This rate compared very favorably with the first observation which was close to once every 120 mins. Other similar changes in teaching practice in the direction of the evidence discussed are detailed in McNaughton et al. (2006).

The following example illustrates how teachers changed their checking processes. The excerpt comes from a guided reading session with four students involving a poem "My teacher said to read the newspaper – so I did" by Pauline Cartwright. (School Journal, Learning Media). In this example, after the first student made the prediction, the teacher directed the group to check that prediction, firstly by referring to a student's previous statement, and secondly by guiding students to look at the title of the poem.

· *Teacher:*   *... What do you think Pauline Cartwright's trying to tell us in this poem?*
  Student 1:   *About war and how people die.*
  Teacher: *Could be. Think a little about what Willie said earlier on.*
  Student 2:   *The newspaper's horrible to read.*
  Teacher: *The newspaper's horrible to read. Look at the title of the poem. Read the title of the poem to me. [They read title]*

Students' reading comprehension results in the next round of testing appeared to reflect the changes in teachers' practices. Firstly, the test showed that students had gained approximately 9 months of achievement in addition to the nationally expected gain over 2 academic years (Lai, McNaughton, MacDonald and Farry, 2005). Secondly, the greatest gain in subtests was made on the cloze passage (McNaughton et al., 2006).

Example 2: Discovering Whether Students Retain Learning over the Summer Holidays

The gains in achievement made over the course of the academic year led to a new concern that these hard-won gains would be lost after the long, 6-week summer holiday between academic years (Lai et al., 2004a). School leaders' concerns were based, in part, on their knowledge of research which suggested a 'summer' effect in which achievement scores, especially of children in lower socioeconomic and minority communities, reduce from the end of one school year to the beginning of the next (Cooper, Valentine, Charlton and Melson, 2003; Heyns, 1978). A local reading comprehension test manual (Reid and Elley, 1991) also advised teachers to consider a possible drop in achievement after the holidays. Although school leaders were already supporting several family-based and community-based literacy programs including a library holiday program, they wanted to know if they needed to develop additional programs to minimize loss over the holidays.

Part of the intervention by the researchers encouraged school leaders to engage critically with the research, rather than accept it as indisputable fact. This critical look was based primarily on the work of Robinson and Lai (2006) and Richardson (1990), who advocate that significant improvements to practice require practitioners to examine the evidence in research *and* practice rather than privilege one type of evidence over the other. In this case, teachers could not assume that the research evidence applied to their context. Rather, they needed to search for their own evidence to verify this effect in their setting.

An administrator opened the dialogue on the possible summer effect by suggesting that the research on the summer effect appeared to be at odds with the evidence collected from his own school.

The research we had looked at suggested that there would be a drop in scores over the holidays. However, our school data disputed that. ... There were a lot of variables that

*could have accounted for our school data not dropping, for example, roll growth. So
I raised the question, "I wonder why ours hasn't dropped?" to the group.[1]*

It would have been appealing (and easy) for the administrator to interpret that data
as a direct result of his school's special efforts to sustain the gains made. But his
refusal to accept an interpretation that was most favorable to his school showed his
commitment to developing a deeper understanding. Instead, he posed this apparent
contradiction between the reported research and the evidence from his school as an
issue for the professional learning community to solve by asking the group to come
up with their interpretations of his evidence.

The community began by posing the question: "Is there a drop in achievement
from the end of the year to the beginning of the new year?" They undertook a com-
parative analysis of the achievement results of the same students at the end of the
academic year and the beginning of the following one. No overall decrease was
evident. In two grade levels, students maintained the gains made and in one grade
level, their scores were significantly better than the previous year. There was only
one grade level, year six, where there was a significant decrease in scores (year six
students are, on average, 10 years old). Overall, these results indicated that, unlike
the published research, improvements made throughout the year, for the most part,
had been maintained or built on (see Fig. 2.2).

Outcomes: By valuing this kind of systematic and evidence-based understanding, the whole professional learning community benefited from the administrator's

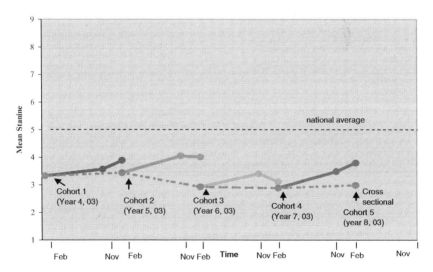

Fig. 2.2 Mean stanine scores for test by cohort and time of testing

---

[1] Conversation from Lai et al. (2004a).

inquiry. Given that the usual explanation for the drop over the summer holidays is family, social and cultural practices and the differential exposure children might have to literacy-related experiences, it appeared that community literacy and language-related practices in which children participated provided a basis for the continuing development of reading comprehension (Cooper et al., 2003). This evidence indicated that there was probably some benefit in continuing to support and promote family and community literacy programs but that the schools should concentrate their efforts on raising achievement within the school year.

The difference between the year six cohort and the other students, however, raised new questions. Why was the cohort so different from the others and how should the schools adapt their programs? As indicated in the introductory chapter to this book, revisiting an issue can lead to more focused investigations and better questions. The understanding of the summer effect had led to a series of further questions about how to support the year six students.

Example 3: Inquiring into the Slump in Achievement for Year Six Students

The professional learning community began addressing this question by adopting the position that a series of questions from a range of perspectives had to be considered to understand the data. They also recognized, based on previous professional development in their initiative, that it was not useful merely to debate different perspectives but that they needed to seek out evidence to understand these different perspectives (Robinson and Lai, 2006). This could lead to conflict, where leaders in the community take the posing of alternate, and maybe even conflicting, positions as "personal attacks" rather than opportunities to clarify understanding of the issue. It was at this stage that previous work with the professional learning communities on learning conversations, which had already established how such conversations took place, was important (see Robinson and Lai, 2006 for details).

The question raised was: "Why is there a slump in achievement in year six over the summer?" The professional learning communities debated many possibilities, three of which are illustrated in the following conversations. An example conversation follows:

> *Teacher 1:*   *Is the slump due to the transition from year six to seven? Some students move from contributing primaries to intermediate schools[2].*
>
> *Stuart:*   *Good hypothesis. The developmental literature on transitions suggests that there can be disruptions in learning when you transition from one setting to another, if settings are not well coordinated in terms of processes of teaching and learning and other features of unfamiliarity. However, we only examined the same students moving from year six to seven in the same schools.*

---

[2] In New Zealand, there are two kinds of primary schools, "contributing" primary schools (years one to six) that send their students to intermediate schools (years seven and eight), and "full" primaries, which have students from years one to eight.

Teacher 2:	*Maybe it's the test? In years four to six, STAR consists of four subtests. At year seven, the test adds two extra subtests. The decrease in scores could be because of the two extra subtests, which may have been unfamiliar to students. I think they would struggle more with the fifth subtest on emotive language.*
Mei:	*The evidence to test your idea is to conduct a subtest analysis of the scores at the end of year six and at the beginning of year seven. You would be right if students do worse in the extra subtests. Let's examine the results.*
Teacher 3:	*Results show that there was a drop in scores for every subtest. So students experienced more difficulties in all the subtests of STAR, not just the new ones!*
Teacher 2:	*The number of questions for each subtest also increased at year seven. Maybe that's the reason?*
Teacher 3:	*That's certainly likely. The STAR test norms show a national drop between those year levels as well.*
Mei:	*Yes, but we cannot entirely discount the fact that drop would have occurred if the same students completed a similar test of reading. Let's look at our other test of reading comprehension the PATs [Progressive Achievement Tests] that we did during the same timeframe. We know that the tests are strongly correlated and this test does not increase the number of questions from year six to seven. I conducted an analysis of PATs to examine significant differences in scores. The test showed the same drop in year six and no drop for the rest of the year levels. Since the PATs show the same pattern, it is less likely that including the additional subtest questions resulted in the drop in scores.*

The example conversation illustrates two important points. Firstly, engaging in such conversations requires rich knowledge about the evidence being examined, including how it has been gathered and analyzed. The community had good knowledge about the assessment and features of the assessment that could account for patterns in achievement, and how the assessment information had been gathered and analyzed. Secondly, searching for evidence eschews early closure. The community deliberately searched for other evidence to disconfirm their preferred hypotheses.

Outcomes: Despite all the detective work by the community, they are still not sure of the best explanation for the slump, although recent data from the intervention suggest it may be an artifact of tests rather than an actual decrease in student performance. This makes it hard for school leaders in the community to know how to intervene because they are still unable to verify what is causing the drop in scores. These leaders will have to continue to demonstrate an inquiry habit of mind, by tolerating ambiguity and reserving judgment until there is more evidence to gain clarity about these results. However, reserving judgment does not mean paralysis of action. A school facilitator of the professional learning community described what her school had done with this information:

At the beginning of the year, our school looked at the year seven results, which were low, and asked the question "Was the result expected?" Teachers said that it was expected because of students' home background. Their initial theory of the problem was that they believed that it was ok for the students to do poorly. Then we looked at the year six results from the previous year to check our theory and realized that we shouldn't expect such results because students did well in year six. Even if this is a national slump, we shouldn't expect it and we should do something about it. Once we realized this, we set about changing what we did. … We even talked to students about the drop. One girl who dropped two *stanines was horrified. So she worked really hard and is now one stanine higher than she was at the end of year six. The slump is not inevitable[3].*

Enablers

The examples illustrate a professional learning community willing and knowledgeable enough to raise and discuss issues. But this was not an overnight phenomenon. The evidence-based conversations were, amongst other things, the result of educative and co-constructed partnerships between researchers, Ministry of Education officials and practitioners (school leaders and teachers), training in the use and interpretation of evidence and a desire by practitioners to put their students' needs above their own comfort. These practices and attitudes had developed over a period of 5 years prior to this intervention, and these skills continue to develop. One of the school leaders has written a paper, from a practitioner's perspective, about the need to develop inquiry in their community of schools (Mose and Annan, 2003); a policymaker has developed a model of the kinds of researcher–Ministry of Education–practitioner partnerships in developing such a culture of inquiry amongst schools (Annan and Robinson, 2005).

The establishment of the professional learning communities featured in this chapter is discussed in greater detail in Robinson and Lai (2006). In this section we will briefly consider two important enablers to developing evidence-based discussions within such communities.

External Partnerships to Develop Inquiry with Schools

Research evidence in New Zealand suggests that many practitioners need support to develop the required inquiry skills and knowledge to engage in evidence-based conversations. For example, in a study of 26 New Zealand schools, Robinson, Phillips and Timperley (2002) showed that whilst school leaders collected a lot of student achievement data, they seldom used them to evaluate their teaching programs. These researchers suggested that this lack of use was due to school leaders' limited knowledge of how to draw the implications for literacy teaching. The limitations of this knowledge, in turn, restricted the learning that was possible from data on student achievement. Similar studies in the UK and the USA show that schools need technical and theoretical help in learning from both externally and internally generated data (e.g., Firestone, Fitz and Broadfoot, 1999; Little, 1999; Louis and Kruse, 1998).

In our examples above, the need for external partners was recognized by teachers and school leaders who actively sought partners to assist them to develop such knowledge (see Mose and Annan, 2003). They employed a researcher-developer to

---

[3] Conversations from Lai et al. (2004a).

develop their inquiry skills, and then sought researchers to support them develop a research–practice collaboration to raise achievement because they recognized that they could not have done so on their own. The elected chairperson of the initiative explained:

> The goal was to raise achievement, and unless we were able to inquire into the causes underlying the lack of achievement, we were just going to perpetuate what we'd been doing. We could say the words, but we didn't know what the problem was. We needed someone who would challenge what we kept saying was the problem and what we were doing about the problem. We couldn't have done it on our own … we needed a teacher, an analyst, a problem solver, a research literate individual. … We needed someone to challenge our assumptions, develop our skills in using achievement information, expand our thinking and enable us to become evidence-based decision makers.

The leader of the intervention we have just described explained why she continued to work with external partners to raise reading comprehension in her school.

> We ran workshops where we invited external partners. The teachers had their class results and the children's test papers. The teachers (with support) looked at what the children were getting wrong and why that was happening. There were robust discussions and you could see light bulbs going on. Teachers were saying, "I can fix that. I can teach them that". The discussion we had with our partners around the data helped. Because it was someone else saying it and not just us – it had more weight; it had more urgency. It made it easier to implement changes because we had outside backing. The reasons for changes were based on the discussed evidence and we were able to use the evidence to design professional development around the emerging trends.

Educative Research–Practice Partnerships

The second enabler related to the nature of the partnerships. Not all partnerships are useful for engaging in critical discussions around evidence and producing the kinds of changes that can support teachers and school leaders to raise achievement. In an early evaluation of the community detailed here, Timperley, Robinson and Bullard et al. (1999) found that partnerships between local communities, schools and government were highly problematic for reasons such as blaming other partners for the educational "failures", rather than attempting to learn together how best to raise achievement. This issue led the researchers to argue that educational partnerships should be founded on the following: empathy for the theories of those involved; ability to offer resources that have the potential to challenge and change the understanding and thinking of those who control the relevant practices and policies; making theories explicit and subject to mutual critique; and fostering of responsibility and commitment by making all parties aware of the possible consequences of choices whilst allowing them the freedom to accept or reject those choices.

In our examples described above, researchers provided new evidence to challenge practitioner thinking, and engaged in mutual critique around various practitioner and researcher theories and hypotheses about this evidence. For example, researchers supported schools uncovering the need to check for evidence, but at the same time, ensured that their theory of checking was open for critique. This also occurred through the mutual critique of explanations in the example of the year six slump, which further illustrates empathy for schools' explanations as part of the inquiry process.

Mei explained it to the community this way:

> *A research-school partnership can easily become a "describe-critique-recommend" situation. That is where researchers come into a school, describe what is wrong with the school from their own theoretical perspective, criticize what the school is doing, again, from their own theoretical perspective, and recommend what they think is the "answer" to the school's problems. In this model, the researchers' perspectives are never open for discussion and are assumed to be superior to the schools. Schools can feel misjudged from this process, oftentimes because the researchers have not fully understood the school context or have based their critique on criteria the school does not value or agree with. What we have done in our interventions is to collaboratively agree with schools on what we all value (raising student achievement). Then we make explicit our theories about what needs to change to improve student achievement and let schools evaluate those theories alongside us. We neither assume that we nor they are "correct", but put all our theories on the table for mutual critique, using the strength of the evidence as the arbitrator.*

Summarizing the Conversations and Outcomes

The first example demonstrates the need for evidence about student learning (in this case test scores) and classroom instruction to answer questions about how to teach effectively. To use a medical analogy, providing teachers with test scores without understanding classroom practice is like providing patients with medication without checking their medical history to know what kind of medication is required. Conversely, providing detailed information about classroom practice without knowing whether these practices raise achievement is like changing a patient's medication without checking whether the new medication is better than the old one! This process of understanding evidence requires teachers to become skilled in understanding students' strengths and weaknesses from a variety of formal and informal assessments, and skilled in mapping features of their own teaching onto the achievement information. That is, they are able to identify the aspects of their own practice which have influenced the patterns in their students' learning.

The second and third examples demonstrate how having an inquiry habit of mind requires asking the "hard" questions to develop a deeper understanding of how to raise achievement, yet knowing that a deeper understanding often means not having all the answers instantly. At the same time, the examples show how these deeper understandings challenge the existing stereotypes and highlight the importance of school leaders understanding the evidence from their context. This is an iterative process, where educators continually seek evidence through increasingly focused questions to gain a clearer understanding of the problem. Evidence in its various forms is selected on the basis of its appropriateness to answer these questions.

There were two main outcomes from using evidence-based conversations as part of our interventions to raise achievement in poor suburban communities of these primarily indigenous and Pacific nation communities. Firstly, we have a better understanding of what it takes to raise achievement in such communities. As a case in point, teachers need to develop their students' ability to check for evidence from a text.[4] We have also learned that schools do not have to intervene intensively over the school holidays to maintain achievement gains made throughout the academic year, although there is still the issue of the year six to seven transition that continues to be examined.

Finally, and perhaps most importantly, we have noted increases in student achievement associated with the part of the intervention where evidence-based discussions form the core of the professional development, both when we have tracked cohorts of students over time (longitudinally) and when we have compared these cohorts cross-sectionally against baseline achievement information collected in the previous year and against a comparison group (e.g., Lai, McNaughton, MacDonald, Amituanai-Toloa and Farry, 2006a; McNaughton, Lai, MacDonald and Farry, 2004). In interventions with two poor suburban school clusters, there were, on average, statistically significant accelerations of up to 9 months in addition to expected national advancements in an academic year, and each cohort had higher achievement scores than the projected level of achievement for that cohort as established by the cross-sectional baseline (Lai, McNaughton, MacDonald, Amituanai-Toloa and Farry, 2006; McNaughton, Lai, MacDonald and Farry, 2005). In fact, in the first cluster (from which these examples are drawn), all year levels and all schools showed statistically significant accelerations in achievement with 52 out of 59 classrooms showing accelerations. Whilst these associations are within a quasi-experimental design format, they nonetheless indicate the influence of evidence-informed discussions about teaching and learning on raising student achievement. Given that the results show that it is possible to change the typical low-achievement patterns facing students in poor suburban schools, the need to then resource both professional development and teacher preparation to engage in evidence-informed conversations becomes a priority.

References

Annan, B. (2007). *A theory for schooling improvement: Consistency and connectivity to improve instructional practices*. Unpublished doctoral dissertation, University of Auckland, New Zealand.

Annan, B., & Robinson, V. (2005, April). *Improving learning processes for practitioners involved in school reforms*. Paper presented at the American Educational Research Association conference, Montreal, Canada.

---

[4] McNaughton et al. (2006) and Lai et al. (2004) describe further aspects of teaching that need to be altered to improve achievement which have been uncovered through this process.

Borman, G., Hewes, G., Overman, L. T., & Brown, S. (2002). *Comprehensive school reform and student achievement: A meta-analysis*. Retrieved April 5, 2005, from The Center For Research On The Education Of Students Placed At Risk Web site http://www.csos.jhu.edu/crespar/reports.htm

Cooper, H., Valentine, J. C., Charlton, K., & Melson, A. (2003). The effects of modified school calendars on student achievement and on school and community attitudes. *Review of Educational Research, 73*(1), 1–52.

Elley, W. B. (2001). *Supplementary tests of achievement in reading*. Wellington, New Zealand: New Zealand Council of Educational Research.

Firestone, W. A., Fitz, J., & Broadfoot, P. (1999). Power, learning, and legitimation: Assessment implementation across levels in the United States and the United Kingdom. *American Educational Research Journal, 36*, 759–793.

Heyns, B. (1978). *Summer learning and the effects of schooling*. New York: Academic Press.

Lai, M. K., McNaughton, S., MacDonald, S., Amituanai-Toloa, M., & Farry, S. (2006, April). *Replication of a process*. Paper presented at the American Educational Research Association Conference, San Francisco, USA.

Lai, M. K., McNaughton, S., MacDonald, S., Amituanai-Toloa, M., & Farry, S. (2006a, August). *Raising achievement in reading comprehension: The effect of profiles of teaching, learning and collaboration problem-solving*. Paper presented at the symposium *Stirring the Waters* at the International Reading Association conference, Budapest, Hungary.

Lai, M. K., McNaughton, S., MacDonald, S., & Farry, S. (2004). Profiling reading comprehension in Mangere schools: a research and development collaboration. *New Zealand Journal of Educational Studies, 39*(2), 223–240.

Lai, M. K., McNaughton, S., MacDonald, S., & Farry, S. (2005, April). *Enhancing the Teaching of reading comprehension in a cluster of diverse urban schools: The role of critical analysis of evidence*. Paper presented at the American Educational Research Association Conference, Montreal, Canada.

Lai, M. K., McNaughton, S., MacDonald, S., Farry, S., Toloa, M., Hall, A., et al. (2004a, December). *Solving evidence-based issues in a research-practice collaboration: The case of the two slumps*. Paper presented at the New Zealand Association of Research in Education (NZARE) Conference, Wellington, New Zealand.

Little, J. W. (1999). Organizing schools for teacher learning. In L. Darling-Hammond, & G. Sykes (Eds.), *Teaching as the learning profession: Handbook of policy and practice* (pp. 233–262). San Francisco, CA: Jossey-Bass.

Louis, K. S., & Kruse, S. D. (1998). Creating community reform: Images of organizational learning in inner city schools. In K. Leithwood & K. S. Louis (Eds.), *Organizational earning in schools* (pp. 17–45). Lisse, The Netherlands: Swets & Zeitlinger.

McNaughton, S., Lai, M. K., MacDonald, S., & Farry, S. (2004). Designing more effective teaching of comprehension in culturally and linguistically diverse classrooms in New Zealand. *Australian Journal of Language and Literacy, 27*(3), 184–197.

McNaughton, S., Lai, M. K., MacDonald, S., & Farry, S. (2005, April). *Plotting effective instruction: Context-specific relationships between instruction and gains in reading comprehension for Māori and Pasifika students in low decile schools*. Paper presented at the American Educational Research Association Conference, San Francisco, USA.

McNaughton, S., MacDonald, S., Amituanai-Toloa, M., Lai, M. K., & Farry, S. (2006). Enhanced teaching and learning of comprehension in Years 5–8. Auckland, NewZealand: Uniservices.

Mose, K., & Annan, B. (2003, January). *School managers, student achievement and a problem analyst: Development of a research culture in a schooling improvement initiative, Mangere, New Zealand*. Paper presented at the International Congress for School Effectiveness and Improvement conference, Sydney, Australia.

Reid, N. A., & Elley, W. B. (1991). *Revised progressive achievement tests: Reading comprehension*. Wellington, New Zealand: New Zealand Council for Educational Research.

Richardson, V. (1990). Significant and worthwhile change in teaching practice. *Educational Researcher, 19*(7), 10–18.

Robinson, V., Phillips, G., & Timperley, H. (2002). Using achievement data for school-based curriculum review: A bridge too far? *Leadership and Policy in Schools, 1*(1), 3–29.

Robinson, V. M. J., & Lai, M. K. (2006). *Practitioner research for educators*. Thousand Oaks, CA: Corwin Press.

Timperley, H., Robinson, V., & Bullard, T. (1999). *Strengthening education in Mangere and Otara: First evaluation report*. Auckland, New Zealand: University of Auckland.

Chapter 3
Structuring Talk About Teaching and Learning: The Use of Evidence in Protocol-Based Conversation

Judith Warren Little and Marnie W. Curry

Chapter Overview *In this chapter **Judith Warren Little** and **Marnie Curry** critique a conversation among secondary teachers in a critical friends group in the USA. The conversation is driven by a problem of professional practice using artifacts of teaching and learning with the discussion guided by specifically designed protocols. These conditions both promoted opportunities for them to learn while at the same time limiting that learning. Through the discussion some teachers recognized and revealed their tenuous grasp of important aspects of discipline content knowledge but the protocols did not provide for this unexpected development. The authors raise the important issue of expertise in facilitation if such protocols are not to take on a formulaic or ritual character that limits rather than enhances professional learning.*

Mid-afternoon sunlight pours into the living room of the home where eleven members of the Revere High School staff – 8 teachers from various academic departments, the principal, an instructional aide, and a counselor – have convened for the group's monthly meeting. The group begins a discussion of student essays brought by Shelby, who teaches a 9th grade health class. Muriel, the designated facilitator for the conversation, opens the activity by reading aloud from a page of discussion guidelines – a "protocol" – as she invites Shelby to introduce the student work. Shelby quickly sketches her mental health unit on violence and violence prevention and the assignment in question: a persuasive essay in which students were to propose three approaches to violence prevention. As required by the protocol guidelines, Shelby then sits quietly jotting notes as she listens to her colleagues discuss her students' work. Early in the conversation, a question arises as Irene, a math teacher, muses aloud, "What comes to mind is how well do the students understand what is meant by a persuasive essay?" Maxine, an English teacher, replies, "Because? What do you see here that would indicate that?" The ensuing talk centers on the limitations of the essays, especially their lack of specificity and supporting detail. Eventually the conversation turns to instructional supports for student writing and specifically to the instructions the teacher had supplied for the assignment in question. The question of whether students understood the nature of a "persuasive essay" continues to punctuate the discussion, culminating in this exchange:

Maxine (to Shelby):   *Do you think maybe the kids did not get that?*
Shelby: *Do you think maybe the teacher did not get that?! (group laughter)*

L.M. Earl and H. Timperley (eds.), *Professional Learning Conversations:*
Challenges in Using Evidence for Improvement.
© Springer Science+Business Media B.V. 2009

The scene above typifies activity in this school-based "critical friends group," as its members term it.[1] Exchanges centered on samples of student work or on the instructional plans and materials brought by individual teachers account for approximately half of the group's monthly discussion time. Taken as evidence-based conversations, these exchanges are distinctive in three principal ways. First, they are driven by, and oriented to, *problems of professional practice* that individual participants bring to the group for consultation, and thus are potentially occasions of what Ball and Cohen (1999) consider learning in, from and for practice. Second, evidence takes the form of selected *artifacts of teaching and learning* rather than aggregated information reflecting larger-scale patterns (test scores, attendance data, survey results) that might be the focus in other evidence-based conversations. Finally, the group formally structures its discussion by employing specially designed *protocols* – procedural steps and guidelines – and by designating a facilitator to help participants make productive use of the protocol format.

Protocols employed in professional development activity define relevant artifacts for scrutiny (student work, lesson plans, tasks and assignments, assessments), establish guiding questions for considering those artifacts, and structure both participant roles and the use of time. Educators have developed a range of protocols that differ in several respects, including their espoused purpose, the nature of evidence considered, the provisions for revealing contextual information, and the intended focus of the conversation during specific time segments. Advocates for such protocols argue that they enable a degree of focus and transparency unlikely to be achieved by "just talking" (McDonald et al., 2003, p. 7, see also Seidel et al., 2001).[2]

Our particular interest in this chapter lies in examining how conversations structured by a formal protocol and focused on artifacts of classroom practice operate to enable or impede teachers' attention to problems of classroom practice. In the essay that prefaces this volume, Earl and Timperley posit that powerful evidence-based conversations require three conditions: the use of relevant data that will promote deeper understanding; "learning conversations" that build upon mutual respect; and an "inquiry habit of mind" to dig deeply into evidence.

Consistent with the organizing strategy of the volume, our chapter examines one such conversation recorded as part of a larger multisite study. As part of that study, we made multiple visits to Revere High School, during which we videotaped the monthly meetings of the "critical friends group" described here. We collected copies

---

[1] The term Critical Friends Group embraces the dual notions that colleagues are essential resources for professional learning and that constructive critique and feedback is what true colleagues offer their peers. The National School Reform Faculty web site http://www.nsrfharmony.org provides more information on the model for these groups. The web site http://www.cesnorthwest.org/cfg. php also provides a description of CFGs consistent with their form and purpose at Revere High School.

[2] McDonald et al. (2003) supply one inventory of the various protocol types and the purposes to which they are addressed; see also http://www.lasw.org for an online inventory and discussion.

of the student work and instructional materials considered at those meetings, together with the protocol guidelines. Interviews with teachers and other participants helped us determine the meaning and value of those practices in their eyes. Our charge was to see what we could learn from educators' protocol-based conversations about student work and teacher decision-making as a resource for instructional improvement.

Protocol-Based Conversation at Revere High School

Virtually all staff at Revere High School (including teaching staff, administrators, counselors, specialists, and instructional aides) participated in one of the school's "critical friends groups." These interdisciplinary groups had been formed as an element of whole-school reform and were intended to promote collective reflection, inquiry, and mutual support. Although the groups functioned in a variety of ways, protocol-based conversation served as one means to help educators establish new ways of talking collectively and publicly about teaching and learning. (For a description of the range of activity across the school's critical friends groups, see Curry, 2003.)

Protocol-guided conversation was a well-accepted and highly regarded practice in the group portrayed in the opening vignette. Teachers volunteered in advance for time/protocol slots during the group's monthly 3-hour meetings and subsequently selected the artifacts of classroom teaching and learning they would bring for examination. Over 2 years of periodic site visits to Revere High School, we video-recorded 12 of this group's protocol-based discussions. Of these, 6 focused principally on refining a teacher's lesson plans and 6 involved consideration of student work.

The conversation we examine here takes student work as its primary point of departure. We consider this to be a strategic choice in two respects. First, we consistently observed across the larger multisite data set that teachers experienced difficulty in focusing on student thinking and student performance even when student work was materially present. Despite teachers' expressed interest in collaboration and in examining student work, the practice of considering specific instances, patterns, and nuances of classroom practice and student thinking remained a largely unfamiliar enterprise. Rather, the tendency was to move relatively quickly away from evidence of student understanding (or misunderstanding) to a general discussion of teaching practice. Second, many of the conversations we observed across sites reflected an impulse to bring exemplary student work rather than work that supplied evidence of students' difficulties or struggles. The impulse to showcase "good work" in turn fueled a norm of sharing and affirming rather than analyzing the work at hand. In this instance, participants examine student essays chosen deliberately as examples of weak performance, and employ a protocol designed to guide their examination of the students' performance.

Using the Protocol as an Evidence-Based Conversation

As the participants settle themselves in chairs, on couches, and on the floor, the group's long-time teacher leader or "coach," Maxine, proposes that they use a familiar protocol format that she characterizes as "the process for looking at student work." Protocol guidelines appear on a two-page handout, the first providing a rationale for the protocol's focus on student work, and the second specifying a time allocation, focus, and process for each of five phases of conversation. Figure 3.1 displays the intended sequence of phases associated with the selected protocol format.[3]

This protocol is of particular interest both because of its frequency of use in this group (4 of the 6 taped occasions of reviewing student work) and because it focuses attention on the available evidence of student work by limiting initial discussion of the instructional context, the specific assignment, or the students themselves. By design, the student work stands alone as evidence of the students' thinking and performance.

Maxine has asked Muriel, an instructional aide, to facilitate the use of the protocol. Prompted by Muriel, Shelby opens the discussion by setting the instructional scene:

Designed protocol sequence	
PROTOCOL PHASE	GUIDANCE TO PARTICIPANTS
I. Introduction (2 minutes)	The facilitator reminds the group of the norms: no fault, collaboration, consensus. The teacher providing the student work gives a very brief statement of the assignment and refrains from characterizing the student or the quality of the work samples.
II. Describing the student work (10 minutes)	The group gathers as much information as possible from the student work. Group members describe what they see … avoiding judgments about quality or interpretations of what the student was doing. If judgments or interpretations do arise, the facilitator should ask the person to describe the evidence on which they are based.
III. Interpreting the student work (10 minutes)	The group tries to make sense of what the student was doing and why. The group should try to find as many different interpretations as possible and evaluate them against the kind and quality of evidence. From the evidence [group members] try to infer what the student was thinking, … does and does not understand, … was most interested in, [and] how the student interpreted the assignment.
IV. Implications for classroom practice (10 minutes)	Based on the group's observations and interpretations, discuss any implications this work might have for teaching and assessment in the classroom.
V. Reflect on the process (10 min)	Reflect on how the process worked. Share any new insights you have gained about the students, about your colleagues, about yourself, about your practice.

Fig. 3.1 Designed sequence of phases in the selected protocol

---

[3] A similar version of this protocol – termed the ATLAS protocol following its origins in the ATLAS whole-school reform initiative – is available at http://www.smp.gseis.ucla.edu/Resourcesforyou/ednews/downloads/ATLAS%20Protocol%20(DL%202003).pdf.

the work she has brought for consideration has resulted from the culminating assignment in a mental health unit "where we talked a lot about violence."

> Shelby: *They see videos. They hear a guest speaker. They have readings to do all about different forms of violence: domestic violence, school violence, gang violence. And then I ask them to write a persuasive essay arguing that there are three ways to reduce violence in society, and they could choose any of the areas and write their essay. And they have to support their essay in two places with facts or quotes from the material that we've seen in class.*

At the close of her remarks, Shelby distributes two student essays. For the next 13 minutes or so, Shelby remains silent and takes occasional notes as her colleagues first read the work silently and then engage in discussion about the student essays, focusing principally on their limitations as examples of a "persuasive essay." As the group turns attention to "implications for the classroom," Shelby begins to re-join the conversation as an active participant, becoming still more active when the facilitator calls for "reflection on the process."

Like many other conversations we observed, this one does not reflect strict adherence to the written protocol, either with regard to the substantive focus of talk in particular phases or with regard to the suggested time allocations or participation guidelines. Participants redefine the various protocol phases, most prominently with regard to when and how judgments are rendered regarding the quality of the student work, and whether or how to introduce additional evidence of the teacher's instruction.

In the discussion that follows, we first parse the conversation with regard to the ways in which the teachers take up the student work as evidence of student understanding *and* as evidence of the teacher's instructional practice. We then consider the part played by other evidence of the teacher's own work – Shelby's instructional assignment and accounts of her instructional practice – at the time they are introduced. Finally, we discuss the overall trajectory of the conversation in relationship to the protocol structure, paying particular attention to selected trade-offs and tensions the teachers must navigate as they employ protocol steps and guidelines to organize conversations about problems of classroom teaching and learning.

This parsing presents certain challenges. The length of the conversation (approximately 40 minutes and 840 transcript lines) precludes our appending the full text and forces us to rely on a narrative rendering of the conversational trajectory. In addition, the conversation lends itself to multiple analyses that take up different aspects of the group's interaction. Most important, the conversation is a vastly complex event. Parsing it as we have necessarily sacrifices many of the contours and nuances of the talk; however, it also enables us to illuminate both the central affordances and prominent limitations of protocols as means of structuring talk about teaching and learning.

Taking the Essays as Evidence of Student Understanding

Student essays – two essays distributed in the opening moments of the activity and a third one introduced later – serve as the principal focus of talk for slightly more than 14 minutes of the 42-minute conversation, or one third of the time. The essays themselves are short, each two pages or less. The participants begin by reading two essays silently. After approximately 3 minutes, the facilitator invites participants to "make observations about what we see" and cues them that opening remarks are to be "descriptions." The conversation begins this way:

> Maxine: I see um, I see um, that the person—it looks like the assignment was—well I think that's what Shelby said the assignment was about. And in the Aisha Brown paper, it looks like the person tried to do—to come up with three ways. [reading from essay] "One way to prevent", "another way to prevent", "above all if we can", so this person tried to come up with three ways to prevent violent acts? But, I don't neces—I mean that's what I see, but I—but the three ways that the person came up with, I don't think are necessarily persuasive or she's not persuasive about them. [2-second pause] They're just three ways.
>
> [12-second pause]
>
> Sophia: [Looking at essay] Part of why she's not persuasive is because she doesn't use any details. There's no supporting example. There's no real building of an argument. Although she's very clear about opinion, about framing questions, she does a beautiful job of that. (What else) am I supposed to say? She does do that. [Puts the essay down][4]

These opening comments set the conversation on a particular course, embodying two of its dominant thematic aspects: a focus on the completed student work as evidence of students' essay-writing skill; and an explicitly evaluative stance toward the work, despite the restraint on judgment urged by the protocol guidelines. The participants articulate a few strengths (e.g., an organizing question in one essay, vivid "voice" in a second) but concentrate principally on what they consider to be weaknesses or flaws: limited framing of a thesis statement, inadequate supporting detail or evidence, muted voice. As the participants consider how to account for the students' performance, their principal explanation centers on what they take to be the students' weak understanding of the persuasive essay genre in general and their interpretation of this assignment in particular.

A recurrent refrain in the conversation, introduced within the first 7 minutes and repeated at various junctures, thus centers on the question of whether the students adequately understood the genre of "persuasive essay." In the opening moments of the conversation, Irene (a math teacher) wonders aloud whether "students understand what is meant by a persuasive essay."

> Irene: What comes to mind is how well do the students understand what is meant by a persuasive essay?
>
> Maxine: Because? What do you see here that would indicate that?

Subsequently, in the protocol segment directed to "interpreting the student work," Carol (a counselor) leads off by suggesting that the completed essay may reflect the student's flawed interpretation of what a persuasive essay requires:

> Carol: I think she interpreted persuasive as just meaning having a strong opinion. (3-second pause) And that's it.

---

[4] For our analysis, we employed transcript conventions (adapted from Ochs, 1979) that marked pauses, self-interruptions, overlapping speech, and emphasis. The transcript has been simplified for inclusion in this chapter.

F:	Mmm-hmm
Maxine:	Ohh, rather than actually trying to convince (me). To actually have evidence to build a case on.
Carol:	'Cause it's very general. It doesn't have any specific like, you know, facts to back it up with.

When the conversation turns to remedies for the observed weaknesses, Irene repeats her query:

Everett:	I think some concrete examples would have made it more persuasive.
Irene:	That's why I was wondering if there was a real understanding of what was required in a persuasive essay.

Throughout, the group uses the essays as evidence to highlight the students' inadequate grasp of persuasion and, in the process, group members surface their own uncertainty about what the genre of the persuasive essay entails.

Taking Student Essays as Evidence of Instruction and Grounds for Instructional Advice

In naming and judging specific features of the students' work and in speculating about the nature and extent of the students' understanding, the participants also implicate instruction. That is, they take the student essays as the basis from which to infer the adequacy of prior instruction and thus also as a springboard for instructional advice.

The third segment of the protocol-based activity, designated as "implications for the classroom," offers a formal opportunity for instructional talk. Shelby, who has been silent in compliance with the protocol guidelines, visibly (and audibly) welcomes the shift to a discussion of instruction:

Muriel:	So are we ready to go to implications for the classroom practice?
Shelby:	PLEASE! (nodding vigorously)
[a few seconds of joking, laughter]	
Maxine:	Well, we can go back to what Irene said about the assignment.
Irene:	I would really want to make sure the kids understood for sure what a persuasive essay entails, and what were the expected expectations of that type of essay.

With Irene's statement, the *question* regarding student understanding ("how well do the students understand …?") has been transformed to an *assertion* – a normative statement – regarding the teacher's instructional obligations ("I would really want to make sure"). Over a 10-minute span, the participants introduce an inventory of instructional possibilities. Of these, one involves an instructional response that builds specifically from the student evidence:

Irene:	And maybe we need a rewrite on this kind of thing, saying, okay, here's your idea. Now let's see what you can do with it. You've got your central idea. Where can we go with it? I sure want to do that with Aisha. I know her, and I know how passionate she can get about some things and—but putting things on paper sometimes is tough.

The remaining possibilities emerge as strategies for whole-class instruction. Absent any evidence of the teacher's actual instruction, either in the form of the written assignment or the kind of verbal "replays" that expose the details of classroom interaction (Horn,

2005), the participants move away from the student evidence to produce a generic typology of instructional remedies: employing models of "authentic" persuasive writing outside the school (newspaper editorials, attorneys' briefs, or courtroom arguments); using templates to structure students' writing; displaying model essays from former students; and, finally, reconsidering the scope of the assignment.

Introducing Evidence of the Teacher's Work

By design, the student essays constitute the only material evidence under consideration throughout the principal segments of the protocol, during which participants are asked to describe what they observe in the student work, infer the student thinking, and consider implications for the classroom. Although the selected protocol makes no explicit provision for introducing artifacts of the *teacher's* work at any time during the conversation, Shelby has in fact brought copies of the materials she had prepared for the assignment.[5] When the facilitator signals the transition to the last formal phase of the conversation ("reflecting on the process"), she also takes the opportunity to distribute Shelby's written assignment.

With the introduction of the teacher's written assignment in this final segment, the instructional talk becomes increasingly specified to Shelby's own instructional decisions and dilemmas. Two central insights emerge as she engages the commentary produced by the other participants, and as the other participants take up the new evidence in the form of the teacher's written assignment.

First and most prominent in the conversation, the students' problems with the essay could be explained by the inference that the teacher herself had only a tenuous grasp of the persuasive essay genre. As a health teacher, Shelby had become acquainted with various essay genres mainly through school-wide efforts to promote writing across the curriculum. Although she had employed two of the instructional strategies suggested by her colleagues (models of student essays and a structuring template), together with other prewriting strategies (brainstorming, concept maps), her colleagues press the question of whether the instruction had prepared students to produce a persuasive essay:

> Maxine: But WAIT, but what are you asking them to do? (3 seconds) Where's the
>   persuasive part?
> Shelby: Where is the persuasive part? I'm asking them to—let's see, so this is the prob-
>   lem of school violence. What are the ways to reduce it? What are some ideas
>   about ways to reduce it?
> Maxine: Where's the persuasive part?
> Shelby: Trying to get them to persuade that there are ways to reduce school violence.
>   Is that not persuasive? (3 seconds) One of the ways
> Maxine: If you—

---

[5] In a subsequent interview, Shelby comments on the particular constraints of this protocol format: "… in my head when I was thinking about what I wanted help with, I wanted to bring the essays that weren't very well done and I wanted to bring my instruction sheet and have the group look at both of those."

Shelby:	to reduce school violence is to have smaller schools. That's not persuasive?
Maxine:	I don't think it is
Lars:	I think you have to—what the persuasive would be is that we do need to reduce school violence.
Maxine:	Or that the persuasion would be that small schools [Lars: right] will reduce school violence. [Lars: Right] Here's why, here's reason one, reason two, here's reason three. [Simultaneous overlapping talk from others echoing "reason one, reason two, reason three"] Yeah. In other words, small schools is a good solution to reducing school violence. Having smaller schools is a good solution to reducing school violence. (F: This is why.) Reason one, reason two, reason three, and here's the proof. Michelle Fine says ...
Irene:	In this study—
Alec:	I mean those are the sources you're citing. "Based on the research done by Michelle Fine." [Maxine: uh-huh]
Maxine:	But isn't it the way in which—I mean did the kids—do you think the kids did not get that?
Shelby:	Do you think the teacher did not get that!?
[Group laughter]	

Moments later, Shelby confesses that she remains unclear about the defining features of a persuasive essay. Asked if she would judge any of the completed essays as good ones, she responds:

| Shelby: | Yeah. Well I think—But I'm a little bit confused myself now about what I'm asking them to do because I think I'm asking them to write a persuasive essay, but ... maybe it's not persuading because that's still fuzzy. |

A second insight centers on the significance or appropriateness of the essay assignment in relation to the teacher's instructional goals. The fundamental issue for Shelby is what kind of writing assignment would let the students demonstrate whether they got the main point of the unit, which was to help them see that they need not be helpless in the face of violence.

| Maxine: | Persuasion is when you're trying to convince somebody [Alec: convince somebody] [Irene: convince somebody] that they can't send ten more kids to our school. Why? Because. blah blah blah. You just can't because it's going to impact this and kids are going to learn less, and you know I have evidence. Smaller schools are better. |
| Shelby: | So, how would you do—what would you, how would you explain it to relating to violence? You kind of get what I'm trying to get them to do is think that there are ways to reduce violence, that we're not helpless victims of the violence that's going on around us. So is that not persuasive? Is there another way to write? |

The Pros and Cons of Protocols for Organizing Evidence-Based Conversation

Our interest rests in the affordances and limitations of protocol-based conversation with regard to professional learning and instructional decision-making. From that perspective, the conversational trajectory, unfolding over approximately 40 minutes, deserves comment in two major respects: first, its steady progress toward new insights for individuals and the group, stimulated by the examination of the student essays; and, second, perhaps ironically, the tendency to subordinate substance to form in ways that may have reduced opportunities for learning.

Professional Learning in and Through Protocol-Based Conversation

The conversation demonstrably yielded insights into teaching and learning. Shelby concluded that if some of her students did not understand the nature of a persuasive essay, it may have been because she did not really understand it herself ("Do you think maybe the *teacher* didn't get that?"). Although she does not achieve genuine clarity about the defining elements of a persuasive essay or how such essays differ from other expository writing ("I'm still a bit confused"), she is positioned to seek additional advice and to think more deliberately about what kind of assignment will best serve her instructional goals.

Further, the conversation arguably created a collective learning opportunity by exposing broader uncertainty about persuasive essays in a school where there had been a substantial professional development investment in writing across the curriculum. Shelby is not the only member of the group to express confusion about the persuasive essay. Relatively early in the conversation, Irene notes that her question about students' understanding results not only from her reading of the student essays but also "because *I'm* not clear on what is meant by a persuasive essay, what are the elements of a persuasive essay." In addition, the students' failure to cite sources as required by the assignment leads Maxine to signal a problem (an "implication for our practice") that deserves broader attention by the school staff – the absence of citations in research papers produced by seniors.

The group's participants, when interviewed, attributed the productivity of their monthly exchanges to their use of protocols to structure conversations about artifacts of practice. In this instance, the protocol enabled participants to transform small samples of student work into evidence of a broader problem of practice. The protocol's built-in constraints on the use of time, the participants' roles, and the available contextual information arguably helped focus attention on the evidence at hand – at least for a sizable chunk of the allotted time.

The Limitations of a Protocol-Based Conversation

Although the conversation clearly sparked some "aha" moments among the participants, and although the group finds sufficient value in these conversations to make them a routine feature of its monthly meetings, this event also typifies some of the limitations of protocol-based conversations that we observed across sites (see also Little, Gearhart, Curry and Kafka, 2003). We highlight three here: the likelihood that participants will privilege form over substance, resulting in superficial examination of the evidence at hand; the potential conflict between "openness" to broad participation and/or multiple points of view and the need for the kind of clarity that could inform instructional choices; and, finally, the tendency for the apparent ease and accessibility of protocol formats to mask the conditions and resources needed for their effective use.

By virtue of their formal structure and tight constraints, protocol-based conversations may develop a certain formulaic or ritual character in which form takes precedence over substance. As participants moved through designated (and timed) protocol phases, they sacrificed opportunities to pursue the kind of probing discussion that Grossman, Wineburg and Woolworth (2001) associate with authentic teacher community. Most individuals made contributions to the conversation, especially when attention turned to instructional suggestions; however, those contributions were generally accepted without question or elaboration – and without requests to cite specific evidence from the student essays or teacher assignment.

Overall, and despite the inventory of instructional suggestions offered by the participants, the guidance for instructional decision-making remained limited. The conversation produced neither closure on the definition of a persuasive essay nor specific resources on which Shelby and others could rely for future writing instruction. Maxine, the experienced English teacher and department head, pushed the hardest on the role of supporting reasons in a persuasive essay, but stopped short of providing definitive criteria for such essays or advice on how (or when) to help students write them. The enacted choices thus revealed the overall tension between the "openness" characteristic of broad participation and the degree of resolution or closure adequate to inform instructional decision-making. When conversation turns to a discussion of the assignment, Shelby concludes: "Maybe I'm really not on target on how to write a persuasive essay, what it should sound like … I have to twist my head around that." At the end of the conversation, Shelby thanks her colleagues for their discussion ("I think this was helpful") but also says that she remains "a little bit confused."

In addition, the apparent ease of progressing through a protocol, together with a norm of broad participation, may lead participants to underestimate the resources of knowledge, skill, and disposition required to make such structured conversations generative. In this instance, nothing in the published protocol guides the presenting teacher in selecting student work that will supply adequate evidence of student thinking and understanding; nor does the "generic" nature of the protocol aid participants in grappling with the subject-specific issues raised by student work, or with the relationship between the assigned work and the teacher's instructional goals. Finally, the written descriptions of each protocol phase make it appear that the facilitator's role is straightforward (in this case, largely a matter of keeping time and reading aloud from the text to mark the shifts from one phase to another), when there is good reason to argue that facilitation is a complex undertaking.

Curry (2006; in press) attributes both the contributions and limitations of these conversations in part to a set of fundamental tensions and trade-offs that the participants must navigate. As they prepare for and conduct a protocol-based conversation about problems of practice, participants confront choices regarding the principal purpose, the question or problem driving the conversation (an individual dilemma or a problem of general interest); the volume of classroom artifacts to consider (student work and/or teacher work, and how much of it); how much context to supply (is more context a resource for conversation or does it close down alternative views?); whether to adhere strictly to the protocol guidelines or to treat them flexibly (does strict adherence become ritualistic or does it aid focus?); how to handle differences in subject expertise and experience; and the value of grooming novice facilitators versus relying on those with training and experience. As they navigate these tensions and trade-offs, participants establish conditions that will enable or impede deep consideration of student work or teacher materials.

Making Good on the Promise of Protocols

Across our sites generally, as well as in this case specifically, those who employed protocols regularly valued them as a means to engage with colleagues in conversation about teaching. In a workplace culture where privacy of practice has long been the norm, such a tool would seem to hold considerable promise for promoting alternative norms of professional discourse and organizing collective attention to problems of practice. Yet as researchers, we could not help but notice the ways in which "doing a protocol" seemed to take on a life of its own. We found ourselves perplexed and disappointed by what seemed to be missed opportunities to consider evidence more closely and to pursue more deeply the questions raised by that evidence.

If protocols are both problematic and promising, how might educators do more to capitalize on their promise? We understand that many conditions may contribute to the effective use of tools like these, including simply the time and space to make use of them, but we nominate three here.

A Clear Focus on Professional Learning and Instructional Improvement Anchored in a Conversation About Evidence

Proponents of protocols in each of our sites saw them as serving multiple purposes: building professional community, advancing a school-wide reform agenda, and creating opportunities for individual growth. These multiple goals struck us as reasonable, but having multiple goals also made it possible to sacrifice rigorous, detailed conversation about teaching and learning to a general sense of "building community." In this instance, group members demonstrated a willingness to expose their own problems of practice to collective scrutiny and an obligation to support one another's professional growth. We argue that community will prove strongest where its members cultivate the habits of mind and norms of professional interaction to talk in depth about evidence of teaching and learning.

Resources of Subject Matter Knowledge and Subject Teaching Experience

All samples of student work represent students' competence or struggles in *something*: in mathematics, literacy, science, history, art, music, or perhaps some combination of them. Similarly, samples of teachers' work represent the teacher's effort to help students learn fundamental concepts or skills in some domain(s). In this instance, the group found itself both motivated by a problem they considered to be a school-wide responsibility (the quality of students' writing) and hampered in some respects by uneven subject matter expertise. To muster a rich discussion of evidence requires that the group members be able to tap relevant subject knowledge and experience.

Skilled Facilitation

A productive balance of comfort and challenge, where we found it, was the product of strategic and skilled facilitation. Protocol guidelines – tools for structuring conversation – help groups get started with conversation about classroom practice, but they are not sufficient to overcome long-standing norms of privacy and concerns about the judgment of colleagues. Elsewhere we have written:

> When we saw evidence of group norms built on open discussion, constructive questioning, and critique, we saw individuals taking the initiative to establish a different kind of conversation – one in which people could push on ideas and practices while still being respectful toward one another. (Little et al., 2003, p.190)

Guides to protocol-based conversations emphasize the importance of skilled facilitation, but also suggest that the needed skill is within relatively easy reach. For example, McDonald (2001, p. 215) writes that "any teacher can participate [in protocols] with little preparation, and any thoughtful participant can move in relatively short order to facilitator." Our observations confirm facilitation to be a crucial resource for these conversations, but also to be demanding in ways that protocol guidelines may underestimate. In this instance, a novice facilitator read from the guidelines to manage transitions but in other ways was unable to capitalize on opportunities or to recognize and manage breaches that compromised the underlying protocol intent. Making good on the promise of protocols thus requires explicit preparation and support for the important work of facilitation.

In the end, we conclude that the benefits derived from structured conversation about teaching and learning likely owe only a modest debt to the structuring protocol itself. Rather, those benefits derive from conversation structured by purposes rooted in professional learning and instructional improvement and aided by various resources, of which a protocol might quite reasonably be one.

References

Ball, D. L., & Cohen, D. K. (1999). Developing practice, developing practitioners: Toward a practice-based theory of professional education. In L. Darling-Hammond & G. Sykes (Eds.), Teaching as the learning profession: Handbook of policy and practice (pp. 3–32). San Francisco: Jossey-Bass Publishers.

Curry, M. (2006). *Opening the black box: A microanalysis of a Critical Friends Group's protocol enactment*. Paper presented at the annual meeting of the American Educational Research Association, San Francisco, CA.

Curry, M. (in press). Critical friends groups: The possibilities and limitations embedded in teacher professional communities aimed at instructional improvement & school reform. *Teachers College Record*.

Curry, M. W. (2003). *Critical friends: A case study of teachers' professional development in a reforming school*. Unpublished Ph.D. dissertation, University of California, Berkeley, CA.

Grossman, P., Wineburg, S., & Woolworth, S. (2001). Toward a theory of teacher community. *Teachers College Record, 103*(6), 942–1012.

Horn, I. S. (2005). Learning on the job: A situated account of teacher learning in high school mathematics departments. Cognition & Instruction, *23*(2), 207–236.

Little, J. W., Gearhart, M., Curry, M., & Kafka, J. (2003). "Looking at student work" for teacher learning and school reform. *Phi Delta Kappan, 85*(3), 184–192.

McDonald, J., Mohr, N., Dichter, A., & McDonald, E. C. (2003). *The power of protocols: An educator's guide to better practice*. New York: Teachers College Press.

McDonald, J. P. (2001). Students' work and teachers' learning. In A. Lieberman & M. Mclaughlin (Eds.), *Teachers caught in the action: Professional development that matters* (pp. 209–235). New York: Teachers College Press.

Ochs, E. (1979). Transcription as theory. In E. Ochs & B. Schieffelin (Eds.), *Developmental pragmatics* (pp. 43–72). New York: Academic Press.

Seidel, S., Blythe, T., Allen, D., Simon, D. D., Turner, T., Veenema, S., et al. (2001). *The evidence process: a collaborative approach to understanding and improving teaching and learning*. Cambridge, MA: Project Zero, Harvard University Graduate School of Education.

Chapter 4
Leadership for Evidence-Informed Conversations

Lorna M. Earl

Chapter Overview In this chapter, **Lorna Earl** highlights the essential role of leaders if conversations around evidence of student learning are to result in a meaningful investigation into how best to teach struggling readers. Through listening in on a conversation in a review meeting that involved a school principal and a group of teachers, it became evident that the teachers had sufficient trust to share and review their student data, but that skilled leadership was required to use those data to investigate their implications for teaching practice. The leader, who was part of a network to build capacity in collecting and using data for decision-making, needed to keep refocusing the conversation from discussing out-of-class interventions to investigating the effectiveness of the teachers' own efforts to assist their struggling learners.

Introduction and Context

Several years ago, a colleague and I wrote a book called *Leading in a Data Rich World: Harnessing Data for School Improvement* (Earl and Katz, 2006). As we wrote in the book's introduction, the ideas within it emerged from our experience of working in schools and districts and our belief that real benefits can accrue from "getting to know" data as part of an ongoing process of educational change and using it locally to investigate real issues in particular schools, as a way of deciding what to do next. We were concerned that schools were being pushed and enslaved by data rather than being steered by leaders, with data providing information that they could use to engage in thoughtful planning and make reasoned and targeted decisions to move towards continuous improvement.

As we see it, school leaders can take charge of change and use data as a powerful tool for making wise and timely decisions that are consistent with the exigencies of their local contexts and responsive to their unique perspectives, not by slavishly applying external standards to their work, or by plotting to ensure that they meet their targets. Rather, they can create their own future through careful planning, honest appraisal, and professional learning, always focused on improved conditions for teaching and learning, as a way of being.

L.M. Earl and H. Timperley (eds.), *Professional Learning Conversations:* 43
Challenges in Using Evidence for Improvement.
© Springer Science+Business Media B.V. 2009

In the book, we used a painting metaphor for using data for improvement. Artists are always driven by data – by the colors, textures, and images that they observe, investigate, and respond to. They use their talent to decide what to emphasize and how to communicate a mood and a message to the audience. This metaphor of school leaders (formal and informal) as artists offers an alternate view to an image of leaders as automatons, using data to paint by numbers on a canvas designed by someone far away. Leadership teams are producers of images of their schools and of their educational futures.

We used this metaphor of educators as painters, working together to capture the myriad and changeable images that matter about their school and present these images to a range of audiences, as the basis for their ongoing decision-making. Sometimes the paintings are completed individually, as teachers or leaders work on their own. In other cases, educators work in teams to create a collage or a mural of their thinking and their work. In all cases, they draw on many sources of information to construct a coherent and distinctive image of where they are now, where they want to be in the future and how they might go about bridging the gap. Finally, educators paint many pictures, not just one, with different purposes, audiences, and issues to consider.

Most painters, even those who appear to be undisciplined and random in their actions, go through a great deal of thinking and planning before they ever begin to paint. Once they have a notion of the content, mood, and image that they hope to capture, they rely on having well-developed technical skills to select their palette and execute the process of painting, all the while making adjustments, changing ideas, and rethinking their vision. Educational teams can follow the same principles when they appeal to data in their improvement process. Figure 4.1 shows the process of using data to paint pictures of school improvement.

Since the publication of *Leading in a Data Rich World*, we have been involved with hundreds of educators trying to put the ideas into practice and to move from data, to information, to knowledge, and finally to wisdom (Ackoff, 1989).

Inquiry Habit of Mind		Data Literacy		Culture of inquiry	
Setting the Canvas	**Planning This Picture**	**Blocking the Canvas**	**The First Strokes**	**The image Grows**	**Displaying the Picture**
What is our purpose?	What do we think we know?	What do we want to know?	How do we make sense of this?	What is included in this picture?	How will we engage the audiences?
What roles do we play?	Where do we want to go?	What data do we need?	What does it all mean?	What will we do as a result of our new knowledge?	How can we show what we have learned?
Who are the audiences?					

Fig. 4.1 Painting as a metaphor for making data-informed decisions

In Ontario, Canada, we have been particularly engaged with a network of districts that have been supported by the provincial government to build capacity in collecting and using data for decision-making (Ontario Ministry of Education, 2005). Each of the participating school districts (13) in one network identified four school teams to be part of a series of three workshops, based on the book *Leading in a Data Rich World*. These sessions held in November 2006 and January and March 2007 served as anchor sessions for the school teams to engage in data use in their schools, supported by a local facilitator.

In this chapter, I examine the conversation that occurs in a meeting of the primary team of one of the participating schools. This team has been considering their data and continuing their conversations about their school improvement initiative through these special staff meetings. The group agreed to run a video camera during their meeting to capture the discussions as they unfolded. The team meeting (their third) occurred in March and was a continuation of conversations that had been going on throughout the year. It was prompted by a review of the data from an individual Diagnostic Reading Assessment (DRA)[1] that they had recently administered to their students in grades 1, 2, and 3. The meeting was attended by the principal, a district consultant with expertise in early literacy and the teachers of grades 1–4.

My particular interest in examining these conversations is to move to a deeper understanding of what it takes to use data in ways that might result in changes in thinking and practice by exploring:

- The nature of the relationships among the team members
- The relevance of the data that they were considering
- The extent to which the teachers were operating with an inquiry habit of mind
- The role of a school leader in the process of using data for school improvement

The Conversations

This meeting of the primary professional learning team began with an update of the data wall for the three grades. This data wall includes the names of all the students in the primary grades and was begun by the kindergarten teachers to give information about prereading skills (letter identification, concepts of print, etc.), and each student is tracked across the grades to indicate their position on the literacy continuum (using the DRA levels as a scale). The data wall also includes information about the various interventions for each student. This tracking system is historical, so there is a record of progress and of interventions for each student from their entry into the school through to the present.

---

[1] This is an individually administered reading assessment that provides information about word recognition skills, comprehension strategies, rates of comprehension, and general reading behavior.

   The principal has organized the school timetable so that all the teachers in each division can meet together once every 7–8 weeks by time-tabling reading buddies (older children working with younger ones) activities that can be supervised by half the teachers while the others meet. It is an interesting aside that the sessions conducted by reading buddies are intensive and focused, using the provincial curriculum documents and training in reading strategies for the senior students (see Chapter 5 by Kaser and Halbert, this volume, for a description of a similar program). The meeting began with a welcome to the district consultant who was attending to provide any support that might be required. The principal then reviewed the school's learning goal – to improve reading comprehension – that was developed on the basis of the provincial assessment and classroom formative assessments – and indicated that 7 weeks ago each grade-level team had identified a SMART goal for their work. Grade 1 teachers were focusing on identifying the main characters in the story. The grade 2 team identified sequencing of events in the story. Grade 3 was working on making inferences.

   This meeting was called to review and discuss the data that each teacher had recently submitted following their administration of the DRA to the students in their classes. The principal gave an initial presentation of the DRA data using charts and graphs she had prepared from the data to show the assessment results for each of the grades, separately for boys and girls. Here is the conversation that ensued.

P: *I have compiled the data that you gave me into charts. What patterns do you think are meaningful? Look at the information. What is your initial interpretation?*

T1:   *There are more boys below benchmark than girls, especially in grade 1. For the girls it is 50/50.*

P: *The majority of the grade 1 boys are below benchmark. What about grade 2?*

T2:   *The boys and girls are about the same.*

P: *I think that's fantastic. We have always had a differential. Why do you think that is? Maybe our strategies in boys' literacy are making a difference. What can we learn from the grade 2 teachers about what is successful?*

The conversation continued with sharing among the teachers about the kind of literature and the teaching strategies they have found to be interesting and worthwhile with the children in their classes. After this interval of celebration and sharing, the principal returned the group to a consideration of the data.

P: *Are there any other patterns that you find? How do you feel about how the grade 1 students are doing?*

T3 (of grade 1): *When I started with the DRA it was a new thing for them. I think they have done more practicing and I think they would do better now.*

P: *Hopefully you will see the benefits of this next time. Now they have experience. We have been using the DRA rubric. Now you will be teaching those skills. We have to take a good look at the data for each child. Don't forget, we improve one student at a time. So, we need to use the data to support all of our students.*

T4:   *I have been sending material home for parents to use. I was surprised that many of them didn't realize that they could be doing things at home, even after I mentioned it in a class letter. Next year we need to make it really clear at the curriculum night that they can help.*

Once again, the principal affirms the ideas and brings the group back to the data.

P: *Yes and we can post notes on our parent portal. I want to go back to the data. You know what is really interesting to me. Look at this plum colour. These are the students who are not at benchmark. It is large in grade 1 and it gets smaller in grade 2 and smaller again in grade 3. We've been focusing on reading comprehension for three years and I think it's making a difference.*

T3 (of grade 1):   *With grade1 it is reading readiness.*

P: *Now the kindergarten teachers are setting SMART goals and focusing on letter identification, concepts of print and things like that, and tracking their students on data walls. So, it might be better next year.*

T4:   *I wonder about the differences in reading at home.*

The group spent several minutes at this point talking about the role of parents in their child's reading. Again, the principal brings them back to their task.

P: *Those are all important things we need to pay attention to as we develop our plans, to monitor our SMART goals and dig deeper to see what we might do. We've been working on literacy for 3 years now and I think we're seeing that working. Any other patterns or surprises for you?*

T3:   *I want to stick up for the grade 1 boys. Although they are below benchmark, they are right at the cusp and it will be a different picture next time.*

P: *You make a really good point. This data doesn't tell us everything. What else do we need to know? What other information would be helpful for you? This general information tells us generally where we're at. Now we know we have a lot of work to do with our grade 1 students? What else would be helpful to know about these children?*

T: *Well—who is in the after school program, in reading buddies, tutoring. Things like that.*

P: *Let's look at the data wall for grade 1. Would you take us through each child and tell us about them. I know it is really difficult to talk about your students when they are having difficulty. It's easier when we are celebrating, I realize that you are working very hard but we're working as a team to see how we can support you. If you don't mind going through each student and we'll see how we can assist you.*

The grade 1 data wall is a record of various assessments and the interventions each student is receiving through the year were posted on a data wall. The grade 1 teachers went to the data wall to discuss the students in their classes. They started by giving an overview of what the symbols mean.

T5 (of grade 1):   *The green dots indicate where they were at the beginning of term, orange are from January and blue are from this DRA. It shows us very quickly which kids are having the most difficulty. And all of the skills are across the top. The stars show who is in the "all stars" (withdrawal reading with specialist). The blue squares are students who are in the after school reading program.*

P: *How did you decide who is in the after school program? I see that it isn't all the children with the most difficulty.*

T3:   *We wanted a small group who were about the same level and looked at who would benefit most from this program.*

T5:   *Now we are going to look at the targets that we set. The red dots show where we thought each student would be when we did the DRA. Unfortunately we fell short of meeting our SMART goals. It was to have 24 students out of 43 reading at benchmark in January. We didn't make it. But some of them are really close.*

T5:	*Here are some of the students that we are really paying attention to now. These are the ones who are below benchmark. I'll start with Carl, one of my students. He came in at a level one, in November, level one and is still at level one. He is getting a lot of extra support but is not moving yet.*
T1:	*Is there a speech or hearing issue with him?*
T5:	*There is a problem with sight but he doesn't bring his glasses very often.*
P:	*I notice that he doesn't have a blue so you obviously decided not to send him to the after school program.*
T2 (of grade 1):	*He's not there because he has a difficult time sitting still and we decided it was not a good match for him. He is below all of the others in the group so he would affect the other students in the program.*
P:	*Have we brought that student to team? With three consecutive assessments and little movement, we really should have others thinking with us.*
T5:	*That is definitely the next step. I'll do the paper work for it.*
T3:	*Perry is another one who hasn't moved this year. I think it might be a nerves thing when he has to read with me. He stammers and makes lots of errors. He self-corrects but he is really nervous and his comprehension is poor.*
T (of grade 2):	*Have you tried sitting beside him in group so that you can listen without being obvious.*
C:	*What about having him read with his reading buddy and you can listen on the side.*
P:	*Try some of the ideas from the group and then do another DRA with him. It may be that he doesn't know it is an assessment.*

The teachers continued talking about each of the students in the group below the benchmark. In each case, the teachers explained why they thought that particular child was struggling, using anecdotes and examples to illustrate their points. In some cases, other teachers had information to add to the discussion. When they finished, the principal began the discussion with her observations and questions about next steps.

P:	*You have done a really good job of setting the targets. They are not that far off. Not quite there yet but sometimes just one level off. They are challenging but realistic.*
P:	*You have talked a lot about after school programs, all stars, all the extra assistance. I wonder if we can help you make a plan for support in the classroom. Is there something that we can do to help you in your classroom?*
T3:	*We are already meeting with struggling students for extra guided reading time during the week. We are also using library, reading buddies. We try to meet with each of them about four times a week for additional support. We use the librarian as well. That has helped out a lot.*
T5:	*We also use the reading buddies, using the same books as they take home for snuggle up and read. We tell the grade 6s what we are working on and show them how to emphasize so that they can really help.*
T1:	*Maybe you could work more with the reading buddies so that they are really well prepared for the time with your students.*
P:	*This is great. More to celebrate. Four times a week. That is excellent. Any more questions. Any questions for the teachers?*

Hearing none, she went on.

P:	*Have you set your next targets yet?*
T3:	*No, we'll do that after this meeting.*

P:	You've been focusing on main idea. When you looked at your DRA charts, looking at your comprehension—90% of the kids have met that goal. You have done a great job of teaching these skills. Have you decided what you will be focusing on the next time that you set your SMART goals?
T3 (of grade 1):	I would probably say sequencing.
P:	Let's look at the detailed results. How many kids are still having some difficulty with main idea and supporting ideas? How many need attention to sequencing?
T1:	Looks like there are seven students who still need attention to main idea. You need to continue with them and make sure that they don't fall more behind.
T3:	Sequencing seems like the next thing to work on.

At this point, the teachers of other grades described various specific strategies and resources that they have used to teach sequencing. The principal brought this section of the meeting to a close by stating next steps and establishing some timelines.

P: So, you will be resetting a SMART goal and take the ideas from the team to use in your planning. Once you have developed your SMART goals we can meet next week to review them and see how I can help you move forward. Thank you ladies. Very well done.

Discussion

The teachers in this school provided us with a unique opportunity to eavesdrop on their conversation in order to understand how teachers, working together, can move towards a shared knowledge base and deep change.

The Nature of the Relationships

As Earl and Timperley mentioned in Chapter 1 (this volume), relationships are a key ingredient in productive evidence-informed conversations that can change thinking and practice. Relationships create a common language and a sense of shared responsibility and provide channels for communication. Respectful relationships depend on trust. Indeed, Bryk and Schneider (2002) found that social trust among members of staff was the strongest facilitator of professional community in a school. They propose that a base level of such trust may be necessary for a professional community to emerge, but working and reflecting together can build trust and strengthen relationships. The teachers in this school clearly liked and trusted one another. They were willing to share their insights about the students that they taught and to offer suggestions and support to each other. This was particularly obvious when the grade 1 teachers were describing their students and the interventions that were already in place. The other teachers were empathetic, encouraging, supportive, and offered ideas and resources that they had used for teaching these same concepts. At the same time, the grade 1 teachers did not indicate that there are any problems to be resolved within their own teaching, and they accepted the suggestions as given, without any sense of being obligated to use them. This is the kind of collaboration that Little (1990) describes as storytelling and scanning for ideas. Although it is respectful and generates ideas, it is the weakest form of collaboration that does not problematize the context or challenge the status quo and push towards rethinking practice.

Earl and Timperley (this volume) refer to a more powerful kind of collaboration for stimulating change – collaboration where relationships are challenging, focus on substative issues, problem identification and problem-solving that goes beyond what is known. Robust and trusting relationships amongst network members can allow them to work together even when they have different orientations and views (Lieberman and Grolnick, 1996) and come to shared new learning that has the chance of influencing classroom practice through a balance of personal support with critical inquiry about present practice and future direction. Evidence-informed conversations can provide the forum for colleagues to address genuinely new, and often difficult, ideas in a safe environment. In this meeting, there was little evidence of the kind of challenge that is necessary for the creation of new knowledge.

This group was very respectful of one another and often offered praise or tacit agreement with others' positions. However, although the principal sometimes asked probing questions and, on several occasions, directed the conversation towards the possibility of examining classroom practice, the teachers were more comfortable discussing the unique qualities of each child and the role of parents in the learning process. None of the participants tackled the difficult issue of investigating their own, or other teachers', practice.

The Relevance of the Data

Using evidence to support educational decision-making can be an exercise in frustration, without a clear road map to guide the process – a mechanism to decide what data are required and how to interpret them wisely. The data review process in this school was driven by the school focus – reading comprehension. The teachers in all grades were gathering data about comprehension from a number of sources and carefully detailing them on their data walls so that they would have a progressive picture of each student's progress and of the interventions that they have received. They also drew on other evidence, often anecdotal, when they thought it was necessary. This process was designed by the team, with considerable leadership from the principal, drawing on the workshops that they had been attending. The data were relevant and appropriate to the decisions that were under consideration. It was interesting that the teachers drew on personal insights and tacit knowledge to explain (or sometimes explain away) the students' progress, especially when the data were not completely consistent with their personal observations. The teachers regularly added opinions and anecdotes, sometimes to illustrate a point, but on several occasions the additions diverted the discussion away from the primary purpose of the meeting (how can the team help teachers work with students in more productive ways) to issues that were largely outside the control of the team (the influence of parents).

The interpretation process in this meeting relied heavily on the principal's talent in asking clarifying and sometimes probing questions. She provided scaffolding activities and ongoing direction to draw attention to the data and to stimulate and direct the conversations back to the evidence and to their purpose and focus as a school.

Inquiry Habit of Mind

Having an inquiry habit of mind means engaging in inquiry and reflection to establish about where you are, where you are going, and how you will get there. It is not a one-shot activity but an automatic way of operating and making decisions that involves turning around and rethinking the whole process to see how well it is working and making adjustments (Earl and Katz, 2003). In this school, there is evidence that the staff members are in the process of developing inquiry habits of mind, although it is not yet automatic. The teachers were becoming comfortable with a cycle of collecting data, organizing them, and using them to stimulate conversation and planning. At the same time, there was no evidence that they were driven by a personal or collective "needing to know" that would be sustained without the principal. The review meeting seemed more like an exercise that happened periodically than one event in a search to unpick the complex dimensions of the struggling learners in their classes.

The Role of a School Leader in Evidence-Informed Conversations

Much has been written about the role of formal leaders in facilitating school improvement by establishing vision and focus, providing support (intellectual and instrumental), monitoring development, disseminating information, and buffering schools from challenges posed by the larger environment. The principal in this school provided direct and indirect leadership by encouraging and motivating others, setting and monitoring the agenda, and providing support and building capacity. She set the stage by using some creative approaches to provide time for teachers to review their data and think together, and instituted a routine cycle of setting and reviewing SMART goals to guide their classroom activities. She also led the team in their attendance at the capacity-building workshops.

Little and Curry (Chapter 3, this volume) make the point that facilitation is a complex undertaking. We concur from our analysis of the conversation within this professional learning team. In this case, the principal also served as a facilitator. She personally organized the data into meaningful displays for the team to consider. During the meeting she played a critical role, asking pointed and focused questions to keep the teachers on track, highlighting the trends that she was seeing, and pushing their thinking beyond their existing ideas. Most of all, she set a tone and modeled a process of considering evidence, reflecting on practice and making ongoing adjustments to practice based on this evidence.

Summary

One of the most pervasive changes in education is the creation of opportunities for teachers to think and work together as a mechanism for focusing and accelerating school improvement in the service of student learning. Whatever the title (school teams, networks, professional learning communities, learning teams, inquiry teams), teachers are meeting together to plan and to share their knowledge. However, when teachers are not directly engaged with the children in their classes, there are always questions about the benefit that this time brings to the education of children.

In this chapter, I have focused on a conversation that took place in one of these professional gatherings. This school allowed us to be observers, examining their work in situ. It is not clear that the work of this group will actually influence the beliefs or practices of the teachers involved. There were still many areas where the conversation was descriptive but not probing, confirmatory but not challenging. The role of the principal was critical in setting the agenda, creating the conditions for the conversation to occur, and, most importantly, asking questions and challenging the group to move outside their comfort zone to address issues and changes that have the potential to have significant influence on learning for their students. This kind of conversation moves towards serious new learning for the adults in the building, as well as the students.

References

Ackoff, R. L. (1989). From data to wisdom. *Journal of Applied Systems Analysis, 16*, 3–9.

Byrk, A., & Schneider, B. (2002). *Trust in Schools: A Core Resource for Improvement*. New York: Russell Sage Foundation.

Earl, L., & Katz, S. (2003). Leading Schools in a Data Rich World. In Leithwood, K., Hallinger, P., Furman, G. C., Gronn, P., MacBeath, J., Milford, B., & Riley, K. (Eds.). The second international handbook of educational leadership and administration. Dordrecht, NL: Kluwer.

Earl, L., & Katz, S. (2006). *Leading in a data rich world: Harnessing data for school improvement*. Thousand Oaks: CA, Corwin Press.

Lieberman, A., & Grolnick, M. (1996). Networks and reform in American education. *Teachers College Record, 98*(1), 7–45.

Little, J. W. (1990). Conditions of professional development in secondary schools. In M. W. McLaughlin, J. E. Talbert & N. Bascia (Eds.), *The contexts of teaching in secondary schools: Teachers' realities*. New York , NY: Teachers College Press.

Ontario Ministry of Education (2005). *Managing information for student achievement: Using evidence-informed decision-making to improve student achievement*. Toronto Ontario, Canada: Queens Printer.

Chapter 5
A Cross-Grade Learner Conversation

Linda Kaser and Judy Halbert

Chapter Overview *Professionals can talk about students and their learning, but using evidence to improve learning is most powerful when those conversations take place among the students themselves. In this chapter **Linda Kaser** and **Judy Halbert** describe how criteria developed with students for improving their reading can lead to meaningful evidence-informed conversations among the students themselves. Through participating in a networked learning community in British Columbia, Canada, teachers developed sufficient understanding of the principles of assessment as learning to be able to implement them in their classrooms. These efforts resulted in the best of evidence-informed conversations in which the students took responsibility for improving their reading.*

Is there any evidence that the use of clear criteria is having an impact on learning?

Pairs of small heads are busy poring over books and criteria sheets in Debbie K's Grade One classroom in Treeview Elementary[1] in British Columbia on a Friday afternoon in mid-May. One of these pairs includes Craig, a Grade One reader, and Elizabeth, his Grade Four reading partner. Craig and Elizabeth are part of a buddy reading program linking older and younger learners. For the last 8 months, the learning partners have been working together weekly. Let us hear how their conversation starts:

Elizabeth:	*Hmm, what was our job today? Oh yeah, we were looking at reading goals. I think we should say the George book is finished, what do you think? We'll read Charlie and the Chocolate Factory. Then you can write about what we talk about when you write in your response journal. I'd like that if someone helped me with my response journal.*
Craig:	*I want to read Charlie and the Chocolate Factory. My goal was to read to find the important ideas and words.*
Elizabeth:	*That's my goal, too. Do you want to be A partner or B partner?*
Craig:	*Which person records first? A or B?*
Elizabeth:	*That's up to us. Do you have a highlighter? Can I use it? I need my sheet. Do you see my duotang?*
Craig:	*Are you looking for the criteria sheet? It's under the George book.*

[1] The authors would like to thank the teachers, principal and learners at 'Treeview Elementary' for opening their classrooms to the authors and for providing the transcript of the conversation between Elizabeth and Craig.

L.M. Earl and H. Timperley (eds.), *Professional Learning Conversations: Challenges in Using Evidence for Improvement.*
© Springer Science+Business Media B.V. 2009

Elizabeth:	Yes, that's it. I need the criteria sheet. Here – let's look. Jessica, are you using a performance standard sheet – today we are supposed to only be using the criteria sheet. I'm going to be A and write everything down today. You'll be B and do the reading.
Craig:	I'm supposed to be telling you my criteria that I am using to tell if my reading is getting better. Do you want me to tell you now?
Elizabeth:	You tell me and I'll circle it on the criteria sheet or write it down. I'll need to know what I am looking for. Go ahead.
Craig:	I'm reading to find the important ideas and words. I want you to notice when I stop reading and talk about the ideas. That would show you that I think it is an important idea. Can I use some sticky notes? I might not want to stop reading, but I may want to use a sticky note so I remember. I like the skinny blue sticky notes, do you have some? Should I get some? Who has the sticky notes? I want to use sticky notes today.
Elizabeth:	I've got some sticky notes. You'll have lots. You don't need to get so excited about the sticky notes. I think that as you read, I'll fill in the criteria sheet with what I notice that you are doing. Then we can talk. Oh, I remember, last time, we were talking about you stopping, chunking the story and then telling me the main idea. Let's get going. I really like Charlie and the Chocolate Factory, too.
Craig:	At the end of the story, I want to tell you the main idea. How will I know if you know the main idea? Maybe you won't know my main idea. Your main idea might be different from mine.

Reformers and policymakers often have large ambitions for whole system reform. The success or failure of all reform efforts, however, must be measured by the positive impact the reforms have on individual learners – in classrooms and in schools. Thompson and Wiliam (2007) argue:

> Learning – at least the learning that is the focus of the formal educational enterprise – does not take place in schools. It takes place in classrooms, as a result of the daily, minute-to-minute interactions that take place between teachers and students and the subjects they study. So it seems logical that if we are going to improve the outcome of the educational enterprise – that is, improve learning – we have to intervene directly in this "black box" of daily classroom instruction. (p. 1)

Timperley and Earl (Chapter 10, this volume) point out that "significant change in schooling depends on the creation of new knowledge for the adults who are making the decisions." They argue that important aspects of new knowledge creation by teachers include developing an inquiry mind-set and engaging in regular, focused, evidence-based conversations with colleagues. When inquiry mindedness and evidence seeking are routinely cultivated, we believe the changes teachers make in classroom practice are much more likely to have a positive impact on learners and their learning. In the spirit of inquiry mindedness and evidence seeking, what can we learn from listening in on the conversation of two young readers?

Our interest in Craig and Elizabeth's conversation focuses on whether the use of clear criteria for reading improvement in sustained cross-grade reading partnerships provides any evidence of greater learner agency and self-regulation. Through this small case study, can we learn about how larger-scale reforms look and sound at the level of the individual learner? Does the use of evidence and clear criteria by teachers lead to deeper understanding and application of criteria by young learners? Does this lead to greater self-regulation and agency as readers? Is there any evidence in this conversation that intervening in the black box of instruction through inquiry and evidence-based conversations among adults leads to stronger learning for individual learners?

The Context

The setting for this conversation is in a small, semirural elementary (K-7) school in central British Columbia. Learners attending this school come from primarily low-income to middle-income families. Many of the learners live in a trailer court adjacent to the school and many of their parents themselves struggled with their school experience. The 22 learners in the Grade One class and the 28 learners in the Grade Four/Five class bring diverse needs and gifts to their school experience.

Treeview Elementary is one of 250 schools in the province that participates in a networked learning community involved in action research for school improvement using formative assessment as a key improvement strategy. Beginning with inquiry is a fundamental aspect of the Network of Performance Based Schools (NPBS). Participants share a belief that an inquiry mind-set helps build capacity in the school for lasting improvement and that a spirit of inquiry rather than the adoption of a specific program encourages teacher curiosity and a sense of agency and increases commitment for learners of all ages. The focus for the inquiry at this school is on developing greater learner confidence through cross-grade peer coaching using shared criteria for reading comprehension. In partnership with Colleen, an intermediate colleague, and with the support of her principal, Debbie has developed a peer-reading program using the older learners not simply as reading buddies; she and Colleen have worked together to develop the older students as co-faculty, who work in a focused way with their younger learning partners in weekly one-to-one reading periods.

Debbie's school has access to quality classroom criteria in reading that were developed and field-tested over a number of years by hundreds of classroom teachers. These criteria, available for teacher and school use on a voluntary basis across the province, are called the BC performance standards. They help to answer the question "How good is good enough?" and describe and illustrate four levels of student performance in key aspects of reading at each grade level. They also contain sample tasks and samples of student work at each of the four levels. Debbie has been using the primary performance standards for the past few years in planning and adapting her instruction. Her Grade Four colleague, Colleen, has been using the intermediate criteria on an ongoing basis with her older learners. The performance standards for reading literature provide the basis for goal-setting, feedback and planning among the cross-grade teams of learners.[2]

---

[2] The BC Performance standards are available at http://www.bced.gov.bc.ca/perf_stands/

The Cross-Grade Reading Process

In the fall, Debbie's work with the Grade Four/Five learners began by introducing them to the "quick-scale" expectations for fully meeting with reading success for Grade One learners through a set of ten lessons, each 30 minutes in length in which they explored questions like: "Who taught you to read?" "What kind of strategies do you use when you read?" Their discussions led to a shared understanding that most early readers feel that they learn to read by working one-to-one with someone close to them, an exploration of reading strategies, a detailed examination of the performance standards and approaches for working with the younger students to enhance reading fluency and comprehension.

The "beyond buddy reading" program had its initial cross-grade session in October. Each session took place once a week, on a Friday afternoon for a 20–30-minute time period.

Reading Purposes

As the year progressed Debbie led a discussion with her younger learners about why they were learning to read. This question led to some highly individualized responses:

> Jessica said she wanted to read to her babies when she put them to bed at night. Brody wanted to be able to read about the hockey teams in the paper with his dad in the morning. He didn't want his dad to have to read aloud to him. Travis just wants to read all the time. He says there are too many books and he has to get started right now. Craig has a younger brother – he wants to be able to read to him every day from chapter books so that he will have a life "in his head" while Craig is at school. Chantel has a moderately mentally handicapped brother – and says it is the most important thing to her parents that she learns to read. It truly makes them proud when she reads to them. She knows instinctively that this is a measure they use to assure themselves that she is okay. Brianna hates fishing and loves to read while the family is in the boat – and she says the day just flies by if she has books with her. Trinity says she doesn't have to do any chores at home when she is reading a book – so she reads all the time! Trase's dad is away three weeks out of every four – but e-mails the family every day and Trase wants to be able to read for himself what his dad has to say.[3]

The classroom context created an environment where this variety of purposes could find ready expression. However, the teacher was also interested in developing the ability of her learners to self-regulate their reading behavior by setting individual goals. Once this goal-setting process was in place, Debbie then inquired of her learners: "How will I know you are reaching your goals?" This led to an exploration of developing criteria as an evidence-seeking behavior.

---

[3] From email correspondence with classroom teacher.

Goals, Criteria and Personal Reading Accountability

From February on, Debbie has encouraged her younger learners not only to set goals but also to think about how they could "prove" to her or an older partner that they had reached their goals. Over a period of a week, the Grade One students identified strategies that they wanted to be able to master. Each student developed his/her own strategy, and then as a class, seated in a circle, each student said what he/she wanted to work to improve. This process led to further discussion because some of the students' goals were strategies in which they were already proficient. They chose goals that were within their comfort zone but not ones that would promote growth. Other students in the class were quick to point out that they had observed that these students were already able to perform these strategies. This then led to a classroom examination of belief systems regarding learning to read. Learners discussed these questions: "Do you take the quick and easy route?" "Do you fine-tune what you can already do?" "Do you take on new challenges?" This discussion led to a whole set of new criteria that was developed for setting a goal:

- A goal must be a new strategy or skill.
- My goal belongs to me.
- You can have the same goal as long as you want, but when the criteria are met, you must say the criteria have been met and be willing to move on.
- You can say you are practicing a learned skill, but you cannot call it a goal.

Debbie, reflecting on this discussion and the process of developing the goal criteria, reported:

> *This whole session actually started me laughing so hard I had to leave the room. It was an incredible conversation between the students. There was a huge range of emotions happening here – indignation, self-righteousness, complacency, "get-out-of-my-face," and a true examination of self. Really this is a conversation many adults would have difficulty participating in because you had to be truthful and face yourself.*

Having examined the issues and debated how difficult a personal goal should be, the class was able to move back to the discussion of how they could individually prove they were reaching their goal through agreed upon criteria. The class decided to narrow the reading goals down to four:

- I read to find the important ideas.
- I want to be able to talk about the story.
- I think about my reading.
- I want to be able to read at the same speed as I talk.

Using Grade One Thinking to Develop the Older Readers as Coaches

Now that Debbie had clarity regarding the individual and collective goals for her learners, she was ready to communicate her new level of understanding with her teaching colleague. Debbie made a chart listing the four goals the Grade One students had developed. Colleen and Debbie then worked together to assist the Grade Four students with generating criteria for each of the four strategies.

Criteria for Grade One Goals

I read to find important ideas.	I want to be able to talk about the story.
• Stops reading to point out important ideas • Writes down or places a sticky note at an important place • Can tell you about the story in a few words or sentences • Might tell you the Big Idea of the story • Discusses what the story is about at the beginning, middle, or end	• Makes predictions about the story • Retells events and talks about the characters • Asks questions • Makes connections • Expresses their feelings or opinions about the book • Stops and retells about parts they have read • Makes inferences
I think about my reading.	I want to be able to read at the same speed as I talk.
• Makes connections • Asks "thick" questions – "Why …? I wonder …" • Stops and talks about what they just read • Rereads if something does not make sense • Gives opinions or expresses feelings about the book • Know something about the author's schema • May infer or predict	• Good expression in voice • Stops (pauses quickly) at punctuation • Reading is at a good pace – not too rushed and not too slow • Not reading word by word

This is the language that the Grade Ones and their intermediate partners are expected to use to discuss their reading skills during the 20-minute conversation every week. But what *do* they talk about? Let us look further at Craig and Elizabeth's conversation and seek evidence that criteria are a part of the learning process.

The Learner Conversation

The two learners, Craig and Elizabeth, have met close to 30 times during the school year to discuss Craig's reading progress. Generally these conversations are 20–25 minutes in length. On this May afternoon a researcher listened to and recorded the partner conversation. The learners appeared unaffected by the presence of an adult listener.

Our analysis of the conversation transcript suggests the following rhythms: (1) getting organized to talk about reading, (2) the younger learner in the lead, (3) older reader takes control (4) mutual enjoyment of the reading and discussion process, (5) confirming the big ideas, and (6) setting new goals.

1. *Getting organized to talk about reading.* As the two learners meet, their initial conversations are about what Craig is reading, why he has abandoned a particular

author and making an agreement that they will read and talk about the book *Charlie and the Chocolate Factory*. This leads to a more detailed discussion of how they will proceed.

Craig:	*I want to read Charlie and the Chocolate Factory. My goal is to read to find the important ideas and words.*
Elizabeth:	*That's my goal, too. Do you want to be A partner or B partner?*
Craig:	*Which person records first? A or B?*
Elizabeth:	*That's up to us. Do you have a highlighter? Can I use it? I need my sheet? Do you see my duotang?*
Craig:	*Are you looking for the criteria sheet? It's under the George book.*
Elizabeth:	*Yes, that's it. I need the criteria sheet. Here – let's look. Jessica, are you using a performance standard sheet – today we are supposed to only be using the criteria sheet. I'm going to be A and write everything down today. You'll be B and do the reading.*
Craig:	*I'm supposed to be telling you my criteria that I am using to tell if my reading is getting better. Do you want me to tell you now?*
Elizabeth:	*You tell me and I'll circle it on the criteria sheet or write it down. I'll need to know what I am looking for. Go ahead.*
Craig:	*I'm reading to find the important ideas and words. I want you to notice when I stop reading and talk about the ideas. That would show you that I think it is an important idea. Can I use some sticky notes? I might not want to stop reading, but I may want to use a sticky note so I remember. I like the skinny blue sticky notes – do you have some? Should I get some? Who has the sticky notes? I want to use sticky notes today.*

2. ***Younger reader as reading agent: how can I be confident you know enough?*** Much of the next part of the conversation has Craig in a lead role. He challenges Elizabeth to demonstrate that she knows enough about the story to assess his thinking about his reading. She is not the least bit affronted and enters into a negotiation with Craig that resolves in shared problem-solving.

Craig:	*You have different background knowledge. You haven't read the book. I don't know if we should just read the chapter of the book together. You'll have missed lots of the proof that I'm telling you the main idea. I'll have to prove stuff to you.*
Elizabeth:	*I read the book – about two years ago and I saw the movie. How about we try reading the chapter, and if we differ ideas, then you can show me your proof in the book. You should be able to find stuff in the chapters you've already read, shouldn't you? How long have you been reading this book? Will you have forgotten? Think, what could help you and me.*
Craig:	*You should read my response journal first. Then you'll know what I've been thinking about the book.*
Elizabeth:	*Get me your response journal.*
Craig:	*Here – read my response journal.*
Elizabeth:	*Okay – (reads aloud, asks him who the characters are) Okay, I'm ready. You wrote lots about the book – almost a whole another book! I think I have a better remembering of the book.*

3. ***Older reader takes charge and sets the scene.*** In the next part of their conversation, Elizabeth seizes the conversational initiative and lets Craig know her very clear expectations for his reading. The sticky notes take on a new meaning as a key link in the reading accountability experience.

Elizabeth: *Here's what I'm listening and looking for.*

> – *I want you to stop reading and tell me the important details.*
> – *I want you to mark the important ideas with sticky notes.*
> – *I want you to tell me the ideas after you finish reading the chapter.*

I want to have a discussion with you about the chapter, so don't forget anything. See my sticky notes! Beware the sticky notes! I have sticky notes and I will be using them. Where's my pencil? I need my pencil to write on my sticky notes.

After you read that chapter we are going to have a detailed dialogue. Do you know what a dialogue is? You and me and we are both going to be doing the talking. You'll be A and I'll be B. You can talk first and I'll listen until you give me the sign. What's the sign going to be? I need to know what our sign is going to be – we'll thumb wrestle – that's our sign – then it will be my turn to talk and your turn to listen until I thumb wrestle with you. Now, let's read. Tell me again, what are you reading to practice?

Craig: *I'm reading to find the main idea. I'm going to chunk, then talk about the reading. I'm going to tell you the main idea. Okay. [Craig starts reading. Reads in chunks, pauses, marks ideas with comments (this is important because it introduces a new character) or sticky notes.] Are you going to know the important parts?*

Elizabeth: *It's okay. I'll make do.*

(Craig reads aloud four pages and uses one sticky note per page.)

4. ***Enjoying and discussing the details of the story.*** In this part of their conversation, Craig is invited to "dialogue about this chunk of the chapter." The two readers proceed to discuss various entertaining aspects of the plot and the characters where they, in a relaxed manner, make connections to their own life experiences. A short excerpt illustrates the nature of this part of their conversation.

Craig: *Tell me what you think is important. I think getting the two tickets was really important. I think it's foreshadowing. It makes me feel really nervous for Charlie.*

Elizabeth: *Well, There were five golden tickets and four dreadful children won them. They got to go the Chocolate Factory. And Charlie won a ticket, too, He was a poor kid – poor but good.*

Craig: *I would like to have a chance to win a ticket. But maybe I would share, too. Maybe Charlie should have it instead of me. He's very poor. I would love to sleep in the same bed as my grandma. I miss my grandpa, and so does my grandma, but I don't want to be that poor. I wonder if anyone shares in this book? (Continues to read)*

Elizabeth: *Oops – better reread that sentence. It didn't make sense to me. Do you know what stilettos are?*

5. ***The coach leads a discussion to examine the big ideas.*** Elizabeth leads the discussion in the direction of exploring the main idea of the chapter.

Elizabeth: *Let's stop okay. Let's try stopping more often and talk more about the main idea. We need to stop and talk.*

Craig: *Oh. How can he have another chance to get the ticket? Did one of the bad kids share? Did he buy a ticket? Did he find one somewhere? Did he steal it?*

Elizabeth: *Well, you've made lots of predictions. I don't want to tell you the answer. I want you to find out when you read. So let's talk some more about this chapter. What do you think is going to be the main idea?*

Craig: *Almost all of the tickets are gone. Should we have hope? Two were found before this chapter.*

> Elizabeth: *I think that there's two main ideas and I think they're connected to the two kids, one who chews gum and one who watches TV. Authors often make the main ideas about the characters and their actions.*
> Craig: *Oh – so I should think about Mike Teevee and Violet Beauregard?*
> Elizabeth: *Probably you should do some thinking about them. Remember, the main characters and their actions.*
> Craig: *I think the main idea is that these kids are not deserving of the tickets. That's what I think the grandparents would be thinking. They would be thinking that Charlie is the only one special enough to get a ticket.*
> Elizabeth: *I totally agree. Okay, let's talk about your reading. What do you want me to know?*

6. ***Coming to agreement on meeting the criteria and setting a new goal.*** As the conversation winds to a close, Elizabeth makes sure that Craig can support how he has met his current goal. Their dialogue then focuses on setting an appropriately challenging new goal.

> Craig: *I'm ready to make a new goal for next time.*
> Elizabeth: *Oh yeah? How do I know?*
> Craig: *I stopped reading when I wanted to talk about a main idea. And I used my sticky notes. I can tell you about the story. I asked some questions about the story that helped me think. I think I got a really good big idea – the kids are not deserving of the tickets. And I can show you the parts in the book that prove that they are not nice – remember all Mike Teevee's guns? I know all about the story.*
> Elizabeth: *Good for you! I think you did a great job, and I checked off all the criteria boxes. You need to let Mrs. Koehn know that you are ready to move on to a new goal. On Monday, 'cause when I see Mrs. Koehn on Thursday, she's going to let me know what your new goal is, 'cause I got to do some thinking about it before Friday. And pick a goal that's already been talked about, okay? So I don't have to think up the criteria – I can borrow it! Anyways, I'll talk to you on Monday – choose from the grade three performance standards – no easy stuff for you!*
> Craig: *I'm doing really good.*
> Elizabeth: *Yup.*

Observations and Ongoing Inquiries

For the past few years, schools in the Network have been focused on understanding and applying ideas and strategies connected to assessment for and as learning. Schools have been provided resources (Black, Harrison, Lee, Marshall & William 2003, *Assessment for Learning, Putting it into Practice*; Earl, 2004, *Assessment as Learning*; Earl and Katz, 2006, *Rethinking Classroom Assessment with Purpose in Mind*; Clarke, 2005, *Formative Assessment in Action*) and are expected to try out some new strategies and be prepared to discuss their findings with colleagues at network meetings.

As we reviewed the transcript of the conversation between Craig and Elizabeth, we asked ourselves the question: "Is there any evidence in the learner conversation to suggest that the emphasis on developing teacher knowledge about assessment for learning through extended classroom-based inquiry is having an impact?" While recognizing that one short conversation between two learners provides a very small view into the learning world of Debbie and Colleen's classrooms, we think that there are some observations that are reasonable to make. We have organized the thinking about formative assessment into three "big ideas" and adapted the five general key strategies identified by Wiliam into six strategies appropriate to the context of BC schools.

What follows reflects the major ideas and the key strategies the teachers have been thinking about and the evidence we can see from this conversation about the possible impact that teacher inquiry, collaboration and growing knowledge are having on learners.

Big ideas	Conversation excerpts/evidence	
Metacognition for learners Learner self-coaching through learning self-assessment is the goal of deep learning work (Earl, 2006).	*Craig:*	*I'm ready to make a new goal for next time.*
	Elizabeth:	*Oh yeah? How do I know?*
	Craig:	*I stopped reading when I wanted to talk about a main idea. And I used my sticky notes. I can tell you about the story. I asked some questions about the story that helped me think. I think I got a really good big idea – the kids are not deserving of the tickets. And I can show you the parts in the book that prove that they are not nice – remember all Mike Teevee's guns? I know all about the story.*
Nimble and responsive teaching Teachers need to practice nimble and responsive planning and teaching to make formative assessment and learning a way of life (Wiliam, 2006). **Inquiry mindedness as a way of learning life** Inquiry mindedness – using thoughtful strategies and then looking for evidence of deeper learning – is a necessity for learners, teachers and leaders.	To prepare and scaffold for the kind of learning partnership experienced by Elizabeth and Craig, both Debbie and Colleen planned extensively together and adapted their planning as individual learners met their goals. By May, when this conversation took place, Debbie was confident enough with the progress of her Grade One learners to involve them in the development of specific criteria for their individual goals.	
	Craig:	*You have different background knowledge. You haven't read the book. I don't know if we should just read the chapter of the book together. You'll have missed lots of the proof that I'm telling you the main idea. I'll have to prove stuff to you.*

(continued)

(continued)

Big ideas	Conversation excerpts/evidence	
	Elizabeth:	*I read the book – about two years ago and I saw the movie. How about we try reading the chapter, and if we differ ideas, then you can show me your proof in the book. You should be able to find stuff in the chapters you've already read, shouldn't you? How long have you been reading this book? Will you have forgotten? Think, what could help you and me.*
	Craig:	*You should read my response journal first. Then you'll know what I've been thinking about the book.*
Key strategies	*Craig:*	*I want to read Charlie and the Chocolate Factory. My goal is to read to find the important ideas and words.*
1. Provide learners with clarity about and understanding of the learning intentions of the work being done.		
This means that learners should be able to tell someone else in their own words what the learning intentions are and how they connect to life beyond school.	*Elizabeth:*	*That's my goal, too.*
	Craig:	*I'm supposed to be telling you my criteria that I am using to tell if my reading is getting better. Do you want me to tell you now?*
	Craig:	*I'm reading to find the important ideas and words. I want you to notice when I stop reading and talk about the ideas. That would show you that I think it is an important idea.*
2. Provide to, and codevelop with, learners the criteria for success.	*Elizabeth:*	*Here's what I'm listening and looking for.*
This means that learners have clear criteria for quality and know what part they are aiming to get better at.		

– *I want you to stop reading and tell me the important details*
– *I want you to mark the important ideas with sticky notes*
– *I want you to tell me the ideas after you finish reading the chapter.*

I want to have a discussion with you about the chapter, so don't forget anything. See my sticky notes! Beware the sticky notes! I have sticky notes and I will be using them. Where's my pencil? I need my pencil to write on my sticky notes.

(continued)

(continued)

Big ideas	Conversation excerpts/evidence	
	After you read that chapter we are going to have a detailed dialogue. Do you know what a dialogue is? You and me and we are both going to be doing the talking. You'll be A and I'll be B. You can talk first and I'll listen until you give me the sign. What's the sign going to be? I need to know what our sign is going to be – we'll thumb wrestle – that's our sign – then it will be my turn to talk and your turn to listen until I thumb wrestle with you. Now, let's read. Tell me again, what are you reading to practice?	
	Craig:	*I'm reading to find the main idea. I'm going to chunk, then talk about the reading. I'm going to tell you the main idea.*
3. Provide regular, thoughtful feedback that moves learning forward for the individual learner. This means that, over time, learners get used to knowing how to improve.	*Elizabeth:*	*I think that there's two main ideas and I think they're connected to the two kids, one who chews gum and one who watches TV. Authors often make the main ideas about the characters and their actions.*
	Craig:	*Oh – so I should think about Mike Teevee and Violet Beauregard?*
	Elizabeth:	*Probably you should do some thinking about them. Remember, the main characters and their actions.*
4. Design and use thoughtful classroom questions to lead discussions that generate evidence of learning. This means that learners practice being ready to think and know that "no hands up" and individual responsibility for thinking about the question are regular parts of learning life. It also means that teachers work together ahead of time to develop strong questions to use part-way through a learning sequence.	In preparation for the partner reading sessions, Debbie works with the Grade Fours to help them develop the kinds of skills necessary to pose useful questions to their reading partner.	
	Elizabeth:	*Well, you've made lots of predictions. I don't want to tell you the answer. I want you to find out when you read. So let's talk some more about this chapter. What do you think is going to be the main idea?*
5. Put learners to work as learning/ teaching resources for each other. This means that learners know strategies and have internalized quality criteria so that they can be productive with their same age and older and younger learning colleagues.	*Elizabeth:*	*Good for you! I think you did a great job, and I checked off all the criteria boxes. You need to let Mrs. Koehn know that you are ready to move on to a new goal. On Monday, 'cause when I see Mrs. Koehn on Thursday, she's going to let me know what your new goal is, cause I got to do some thinking about it*

(continued)

(continued)

Big ideas	Conversation excerpts/evidence	
		before Friday. And pick a goal that's already been talked about, okay? So I don't have to think up the criteria – I can borrow it! Anyways, I'll talk to you on Monday – choose from the grade three performance standards – no easy stuff for you!
6. Do everything you can think of to make sure that learners are the owners of their own learning. This means that learners are genuinely engaged in learning and confident that they can learn and think about their own learning.	*Craig:*	*I'm ready to make a new goal for next time.*
	Elizabeth:	*Oh yeah? How do I know?*
	Craig:	*I stopped reading when I wanted to talk about a main idea. And I used my sticky notes. I can tell you about the story. I asked some questions about the story that helped me think. I think I got a really good big idea – the kids are not deserving of the tickets. And I can show you the parts in the book that prove that they are not nice – remember all Mike Teevee's guns? I know all about the story.*

Reflections

Elmore (2002, 2003) and others have been persuasive about the need for educators to focus their change efforts in the areas that actually make a difference to individual student learning. We are interested in learning more about how to answer the question of what classrooms look like and sound like when regular learner-to-learner, inquiry-oriented conversations are a way of life.

After considerable reflection on the dialogue between these two young learners, we suggest that an additional way of thinking – and moving to action – about learning improvements resides in creating environments where older learners acquire the strategies and the motivation to work in a focused way with younger learners. Within this type of learning environment, both older and younger learners can practice and develop inquiry-oriented and evidence-seeking habits of mind. Perhaps our challenge, in addition to "creating new knowledge for the adults who are making the decisions" as suggested by Earl and Timperley (Chapter 1, this volume), is also to put emerging knowledge into use. A key challenge is using the knowledge currently being generated in the areas of self-regulated learning and formative assessment to assist teachers to make such practices a way of life. Business writers Pfeffer and Sutton (2000) have written convincingly about the challenges involved in closing the knowing–doing gap. They argue that closing the knowing–doing gap is more important than closing the gap between ignorance and knowing.

We see evidence in this conversation that the use of clear criteria for reading improvement has been internalized in the literacy practice of these two young readers. The individualized nature of the goal-setting, evidence seeking and use of a set of clear criteria that provide both content and process knowledge for reading success makes it more likely that these two learners are acquiring greater learner agency and the habits of self-regulation. Contrasting their strategy use with work being done with secondary learners in an ongoing study of learner self-regulation in classrooms in British Columbia and Quebec (Cartier, Butler and Janoz, 2006) would suggest that these two readers have made a very productive start on a set of strategies that some adolescent literacy learners have yet to develop. Craig appears to set personal goals quite confidently. He has a strategy for monitoring his learning that he can articulate to his reading partner and he controls, in a negotiated way, his motivation for reading comprehension. In this conversation he seems to exhibit many of the characteristics of a self-regulated learner and he clearly enjoys the interactive conversation about a book that would generally be considered quite a challenge for a Grade One male reader.

An interesting avenue of inquiry regarding Craig and other young readers is the role that the "tools of the thinking trade" play in making partnerships and conversations productive. In this single case, for example, the "skinny blue stick its" and the ready availability to the learners of the performance standards criteria in a partnership duotang seemed to play an important role in organizing the learning tasks and making the evidence of reading strategies readily available for use. In the terms of Kanter's (2004) view about the importance of confidence in creating winning streaks, we might even go so far as to suggest that the partnership between Elizabeth and Craig is contributing in a positive way to Craig being on a "winning streak" in his literacy comprehension practice. The conversation seems to point in the direction of what occurs in winning streaks:

> that individuals can perform miracles, that they do indeed walk on water. But every water walker needs the stones to make it possible to move across the water. Knowing that what's underneath will hold you and help you rise to victory is the essence of confidence. (p. 369)

If similar recorded learning partner conversations provide additional evidence that clear criteria, strategies and a well-prepared learning partner create learner confidence, we might reasonably argue that these conditions create the foundation "stones" to support young readers as they develop personal reading strength. This may stretch the implications of this conversation too far. What can be reasonably suggested, however, is that learning rather than fixed mind-sets (Dweck, 2006) are evident in the language and behavior of both these young readers. When thoughtful criteria are made available to, and internalized by, primary and intermediate-age learners who work in learning partnerships, greater self-regulation and pleasure in reading can reasonably be assumed to result.

Perhaps when the shift to a "narrative of inquiry" that Ball and Cohen (1999) called for in their examination of teacher professional practice becomes a way of life for cross-grade learners examining their evolving literacy practices, our research lens can move appropriately even closer to the learning action. Ball and

Cohen created a blueprint for developing practice and practitioners that, if put in place, would replace a "rhetoric of conclusions" with "discourses of practice":

> *This discourse would emphasize more the "narrative of inquiry." Instead of a definitiveness of answers and fixes, the focus would be on possibilities, methods of reasoning, alternative conjectures, and supporting evidence and arguments. It could legitimate and invest authority in a stance of deliberative uncertainty in and about practice. With such conversations, conducted from such a stance, teachers' practice could be improved by acknowledging the limits of knowledge in practice, expanding teachers' capacity to grasp the nature of these uncertainties, and improving their capacity to manage and learn from them with thoughtful analytic – that is, not purely idiosyncratic – consideration of alternatives. (p 15)*

Expanding the frequency of inquiry-oriented, evidence-informed conversations by learners, their teachers and members of their school communities – as well as by policymakers – would, in our mind, lead to more powerful learning experiences for all learners. Possibly we can draw on the learning partnerships of Craig and Elizabeth, and of Debbie and Colleen, to provoke our thinking as we do so.

References

Ball, D. L., & Cohen, D. K. (1999). Developing practice, developing practitioners. Toward a practice-based theory of professional education. In G. Sykes & L. Darling-Hammond (Eds.), *Teaching as the learning profession: Handbook of policy and practice* (pp. 3–32). San Francisco, CA: Jossey Bass.

Black, P., Harrison, C., Lee, C., Marshall, B., & Wiliam, D. (2003). *Assessment for learning: Putting it into practice.* Berkshire: Open University Press.

Cartier, S. C., Butler, D. L., & Janoz, M. (2006). *Students' self regulation when learning through reading in schools located within disadvantaged neighborhoods.* Paper presented at the annual meeting of the American Educational Research Association (AERA) held April 6–12, San Francisco, CA.

Clarke, S. (2005). *Formative assessment in action: Weaving the elements together.* London: Hodder Murray.

Dweck, C. (2006). *Mindset: The new psychology of success.* New York: Random House.

Earl, L. (2004). *Assessment as learning: Using classroom assessment to maximize student learning.* Thousand Oaks, CA: Corwin Press.

Earl, L., & Katz, S. (2006). *Rethinking classroom assessment with purpose in mind: Assessment for learning, assessment as learning and assessment of learning.* Western Northern Canadian Protocol Assessment Document.

Elmore, R. (2002). *The limits of "change".* Retrieved from Harvard Education Letter Research Online Web Site http://www.edletter.org/past/issues/2002-jf/limitsofchange.html

Elmore, R. F. (2003). A plea for strong practice. *Educational Leadership, 62*(3), 6–11.

Kanter, R. M. (2004). *Confidence: How winning streaks and losing streaks begin and end.* New York: Crown Business.

Pfeffer, J., & Sutton, R.I. (2000). *The knowing-doing gap: How smart companies turn knowledge into action.* Boston, MA: Harvard Business School Press.

Thompson, M., & Wiliam, D. Y. (2007). *Tight but loose: A conceptual framework for scaling up school reforms.* Paper presented at the annual meeting of the American Educational Research Association (AERA) held between April 9–13, 2007, Chicago, IL.

William, D. (2006). Assessment the Bridge Connecting Teaching and Learning. *Journal of Staff Development, 27*(1), 16–20.

Chapter 6
Evidence-Informed Conversations
Making a Difference to Student Achievement

Helen Timperley

*Chapter Overview   In this chapter **Helen Timperley** illustrates some qualities of conversations that were differentially effective in focusing teaching practice in ways that impacted on student learning in New Zealand. The qualities of the more effective conversations between these leaders and their teachers demonstrated an urgency to solve the achievement problems of slow-progress students and the use of multiple sources of evidence to diagnose student learning difficulties. The achievement data were used in these conversations as a catalyst for gathering further evidence to refine diagnoses and develop more effective solutions for struggling readers. Less effective conversations became stuck in activity traps in which examining data and having conversations was seen as a good thing to do with only a vaguely defined purpose for doing so.*

An analysis of the reading scores in seven schools serving students from two low-income communities in New Zealand posed an intriguing question. Why were the students in two schools who had been at school for 1 year reading at significantly higher levels than similar students in the other five schools? All the teachers of Year One (Kindergarten/Grade One) students from the schools had attended the same intensive professional development in early literacy instruction and the usual explanations for the differences did not stand up to scrutiny. The students were from similar backgrounds and had similar reading levels when starting school. Classroom observations showed that the teachers were all able to implement the instructional approach promoted in the professional development, at least when the researchers were watching, and questionnaire responses indicated that nearly all the teachers valued the approach to literacy instruction very highly and felt equally successful in implementing it.

The schools were all participating in a schooling improvement initiative funded and led by the New Zealand Ministry of Education. A report by the national audit and review office had triggered a major intervention in the governance and management of the schools because over half were deemed to be offering inadequate education (Education Review Office, 1996). A partnership between the schools, the communities and the Ministry of Education led to the identification of literacy as the main focus of the initiative. All participating schools were located in the poorest 10% of

L.M. Earl and H. Timperley (eds.), *Professional Learning Conversations:*
Challenges in Using Evidence for Improvement.
© Springer Science + Business Media B.V. 2009

communities in the country in terms of their socioeconomic status. Their populations were predominantly Maori (New Zealand's indigenous people), and first/second generation immigrants from one of the small Pacific Island nations of Samoa, Tonga, Fiji, Nuie or the Cook Islands. The students in these two suburbs had a long history of low literacy achievement despite many interventions over a period of years.

Under New Zealand's self-managing schools legislation (New Zealand Government, 1989), schools could not be compelled to take part in any particular aspect of the schooling improvement initiative. In its third year, all 35 primary schools were given the opportunity to access professional development funding for literacy for teachers of Year One students. The schools participating in this study took up this opportunity and most students showed improved literacy scores compared with previous years (Phillips et al., 2001). On completion of the professional development, all the schools agreed to participate in a research project on sustainability that investigated what happened in each of the schools over the next 2 years when supports specific to professional development were withdrawn.

Over the 3-year period of the research, principals, literacy leaders and three teachers within each school were interviewed, classroom teaching observed and achievement data collected. In all but one of the schools the teachers appeared to be sustaining the desired teaching practices and were equally motivated to use them. It was not until the teachers' meetings were observed and recorded towards the end of the first year of the research and again in a second year that substantive differences between them became evident. The qualities of the conversations among the teachers and their literacy leaders and how those conversations related to the evidence of student learning differentiated the two groups of schools. These conversations, in turn, impacted on teachers' expectations of themselves as able to make a difference to their students' progress in reading, and how they approached the learning difficulties of the students in their classrooms (Timperley and Wiseman, 2003).

During the professional development the teachers and their literacy leaders were encouraged to meet regularly to discuss any issues that arose when implementing the approach to literacy instruction. All the schools continued with these meetings after the course had finished, but even at this organizational level differences were apparent. In the two schools with higher student achievement, regular review meetings were scheduled. In one school these meetings occurred twice per school term, in the other they took place once per school term. Student progress on reading and writing assessments, together with an analysis of teaching practices that might inhibit or promote such progress, formed the basis of discussion. In the other five schools, meetings to discuss literacy were held more irregularly and/or informally. Rather than basing these conversations on information about student progress, they focused mostly on teaching practice. It was not that these latter schools were any less "professional" in the traditional sense of professionalism (Hargreaves and Goodson, 1996), but rather they had a different focus for their discussions.

To illustrate these differences, three examples of conversations that took place in the meetings in the two groups of schools are presented and contrasted in the remainder of this chapter. The first conversation is from one of the schools with higher student achievement and illustrates how the three components of inquiry-based conversations using evidence outlined in the introductory chapter to this volume were integrated. The team used data that provided both diagnostic and progress information on students and self-reports of teaching practices. Further data were collected in classrooms when this proved necessary.

The second set of conversations came from one of the schools with initially lower student achievement but showed improvement when they changed their focus and interactions during the meeting. The first conversation revolved around data on student progress but it was not accompanied by an interrogation of that data in terms of its implications for teaching practice. However, when the literacy leader became convinced through project-level data that this data interrogation process was crucial to changing teaching practice in ways that impacted on student achievement, she changed the way in which she talked about the data with her teachers.

The third conversation also came from one of the schools with lower student achievement where the data discussed were teacher reports of their writing programs. However, the conversations were dominated by the idea that teachers should be autonomous in their decision-making and so contributed little to the collective actions of the group.

The Conversations: Example One

In this conversation, the leader and participating teachers in one of the higher-achieving schools demonstrated their commitment to data-informed inquiry in terms of trying to identify why slow-progress students were not achieving and how to teach them more effectively. The leader had been forced to postpone the team meeting for a week due to a conflicting school event. Her frustration is evident in the way she opened the meeting. The teachers had assessed their students using a detailed diagnostic instrument and provided her with individual student reading levels which she had graphed in a way that allowed them to see which students were falling below nationally expected levels of progress. The graphs were compiled for the purpose of guiding ongoing instruction, particularly for those students who were not making adequate progress and she needed the meeting to ensure that the teachers were able to interpret the data plotted on the graphs for this purpose. She began the meeting as follows:

> We had to postpone the meeting until today but I have made the graph available to some of you already … instead of waiting until today because it would have meant that we lost a few valuable days if we waited until today to action this tomorrow. So I have said to some of you to have a look at it and see if we can make some improvement to our teaching, and some of you have.

When the meeting was underway, they reviewed the progress of targeted students identified the previous term to see if the agreed strategies had been successful, then turned their focus to the more recently graphed reading scores. The following conversation during the meeting illustrates how she identified the slow-progress students and remained focused on the central purpose of diagnosing the difficulties and tailoring the teachers' instructional practices to overcome them.

Literacy leader: Let's get on with the reading levels. Now I noticed in [Teacher One's]
                    class that Tama has had eleven weeks at school and he's reading at level
                    two. What is his problem?
Teacher One: He is away a lot.
Literacy leader: Is he managing his one-to-one [written/spoken word correspondence]?
Teacher One: Yes. He's trying so hard at that and he's working so hard – he knows "I",
                    and "to", "I am running".
Literacy leader: "I am running", OK. If he's mastered "I am running", then he should
                    be on to the next level. Has he got the strategies he needs?
Teacher One: One-to-one [correspondence] but he runs out of words to point to ...
Literacy leader: Does he understand it? A lot of these children don't understand it [one-
                    to-one correspondence].
Teacher Two: It's when I ask, "What do you see? What do you say?" That's what they
                    don't understand.
Literacy leader: What? Do you mean that they don't understand the question?
Teacher Two: They run out of words to say. They have no idea what we are asking.
Literacy leader: So I say to them, hide all your fingers – I only want to see one finger and
                    read it with your finger. When they run out of words, then I ask the
                    questions.
Teacher Three: That's what I do for reading recovery.
Literacy leader: While the child is pointing, are you doing this?
Teacher: No. I'll have a try.

Although this conversation focused on a relatively specific instructional strategy that may or may not be effective, the meeting conversations provided a platform for the teachers to continue their diagnoses and problem-solving with one another more informally throughout the school term. All the teachers reported that they sought the assistance of their colleagues in a variety of ways between meetings. They also reviewed the progress of targeted students at each meeting as a way of testing whether the suggested strategies were effective in assisting the struggling students.

The conversation in the meeting then moved to the next two students identified as falling behind their peers. They were both in the same class and the achievement data again was the starting point for the conversation. However, in this case the data were insufficient to diagnose the problem and so served as a catalyst for the collection of more evidence. After the teacher described the problem and found the suggested solutions by team members unhelpful, she said with some level of frustration:

Teacher: I think those two are finding it hard with the level I had them on last time
                    because they were on Level 9 so I put them down to Level 6 or lower
                    than 6. Just up and down on those levels because I don't know what to
                    do with them now I'm having trouble with ...
Literacy leader: So you are asking for help?
Teacher: Yes.
Literacy leader: Do you want someone to observe you teaching the book, or do you want
                    to observe somebody [teaching], or do you want someone to look at the
                    reading strategies in the whole process?
Teacher: Maybe how I can help these two children with their book ...
Literacy leader: OK, so we need some help for you. Be thinking team about the kind of
                    help that we may be able to offer.

The follow-up classroom observation became a continuation of the conversation. The literacy leader worked with the students and together with the teacher developed some alternative diagnoses about the difficulties they were experiencing leading to specific strategies the teacher then tried. The two students then made better progress.

In these two conversations from the same meeting the reading-level scores formed the starting point of the conversation, but these scores on their own were inadequate to provide the diagnosis on which to base instruction. In both cases, further evidence was needed in order to analyze the difficulties experienced by the students. In one case, the teacher's description of what the students could or could not do was sufficient for her to move on from that point with the assistance of her colleagues. In the other, further observational data were needed to analyze what kind of instructional strategies would assist the students to develop the early reading skills they needed to stay on a trajectory of success.

In the introductory chapter to this book, Earl and Timperley proposed that the use of data in an inquiry-based conversation where evidence was used effectively required a clear purpose with interpretation of the data focused on this purpose. In this meeting analysis, the purpose was focused consistently on improving teaching to ensure students kept up with national benchmarks in reading and put them on a trajectory for success. The need for the data to be discussed and interpreted, rather than assuming they stood alone or spoke for themselves, was well understood by the participants.

The relationship aspect of conversations outlined in Chapter 1 has a dimension within it of mutual respect, in the sense of taking time both to understand and to challenge the information and reasoning on which an individual's ideas are based. Mutual respect can be built, or destroyed, through the inquiry process. Asking teachers to present their diagnoses of teaching – learning problems and then to co-construct alternative evidence-informed diagnoses and solutions – is an important part of a respectful conversational interaction. It does not mean that all must agree, but rather that views are heard, together with the evidence or reasoning that supports them, before moving on. In order to learn from the data and the different solutions, however, the process of testing the efficacy of alternative solutions in terms of their impact on student learning is essential, otherwise the solutions run the risk of becoming based on personal preference rather than being evidence-informed. The way the teachers revisited each of the targeted students' progress each term and continued to collect evidence of classroom practice illustrated their engagement with this ongoing learning process.

Mutual respect and learning is closely tied to motivation. It is difficult to judge from snippets of a conversation whether ongoing learning and respect, or feelings of being judged in de-motivating ways, were the outcome. Follow-up interviews indicated that the teachers in the two schools with higher student progress valued the meeting time when they could raise and help problem-solve the students' reading difficulties. One teacher described how the process helped to increase her motivation to work with the slower-progress students.

Teacher: *[The literacy leader] maps them for us and we can see who is falling behind which is good. With my lowest group I see them four times a week and try to push them up. You can see who is struggling and depending on how long they've been at school to where they should be and where they are at.*

> *And you can see where you have to close the gap. So it's good and we talk*
> *about that.*
>
> Interviewer: *Are you saying that when you see a group is below average that provides*
> *the motivation to push them up?*
>
> Teacher: *Yes, because you don't want any of them to be below.*
>
> Interviewer: *I was wondering where the motivation came from. Is it from the others who*
> *know those children are below?*
>
> Teacher: *No, you just want them to do well. You don't want them to come out of your*
> *class not equipped to go to the next year.*

The Conversations: Example Two

This second example provides two contrasting conversations with the same literacy leader and team of teachers. Both conversations were data-based, but in the first the purpose was undefined and inquiry into aspects of practice that would make a difference to students was missing. Similarly, the elements of the learning conversation of maximizing valid information and challenging the reasoning and information on which people's ideas were based were also missing. In the second conversation, the literacy leader was clearer about the purpose for engaging with the evidence, but the difficulties she experienced in deepening the conversation illustrates some of the challenges involved in having such conversations.

The only literacy leader from the schools with lower-achieving students who had reading progress data at the meeting began with a less urgent appeal to the data than was evident in the higher-achieving schools. She began the meeting:

> *What we're going to do today is I just wanted to just very quickly go through the latest bit*
> *of data – I've given you a copy but I know it's a paper war and just have a look at it today*
> *and if you don't want it just give it back to me. You don't have to file it or anything like*
> *that at this stage … it's just hand-written.*

In an earlier interview with the researcher she had expressed concern that the students' rate of progress had declined in recent months. She attributed this decline to teachers drifting from the essential elements of the approach to teaching literacy promoted in the professional development. She presented the data to the teachers in the meeting in the hope that they would notice this decline and come to the same conclusion. When the ensuing conversation did not take this tack, she drew their attention to the decline, but then explained it in terms of large classes, competing school events, student absences and parents being unsure of how to support what they were doing at school because she did not want to upset her teachers. Embedded in this list was the comment:

> *[in] Term 3 we finished the professional development and weren't given that intensive*
> *fortnightly burst of keeping us on track all the time. I wasn't monitoring as closely in the*
> *second half of the year as I was in the first half of the year.*

None of the teachers picked up on her concerns in the subsequent conversation. Rather they contributed other external factors such as unhealthy diets and late bedtimes to the list of possible causes of the decline in results. Unlike the leaders in the teachers' meeting in the first example, this leader did not provide any clear purpose for examining the data. The literacy leader's attempts to promote serious inquiry into their meaning failed because the crucial stage of interpretation focused on external factors and was divorced from the teaching–learning relationship. The following quote from the teacher whose students made the least progress illustrates the centrality of the interpretation process if data are to be used for this purpose and shows how the same data can mean very different things to different people. When asked by the interviewer how she interpreted the progress data, she gave an unexpected reply considering the particularly slow progress of her students,

> I think it's a buzz. It gives you a lift. … I feel I'm doing quite well with my children.

When asked later in the interview what it would take for her to change her program, she replied:

> *Just my own thinking. I'll probably continue until someone comes along and has a look and says, 'Mmm, what are you doing?' and I'll say, 'Well I'm doing that because I think it's best for my children'.*

In the absence of a shared understanding of the purpose of presenting the data, or the meanings that might be derived from them, it is not surprising that program decisions became a matter of personal preference, rather than a decision being arbitrated by the evidence about what is most effective for the students. Many elements of the model for inquiry-based conversations in the introductory chapter to this volume were missing. The evidence was available but the inquiry habit of mind to interpret and act on it were missing.

Following this conversation, the literacy leader became aware that schools in which the teachers engaged with the evidence to identify problems and develop solutions were more successful in promoting the reading levels of their students. She decided to change her approach and in a subsequent meeting she presented the data this way:

> *This is a valuable time – collecting all that data in and just looking at it. Although it is a pain getting it ready, it is the only way we are going to make a difference. I will give it out to you in a minute and you can have a look to see in your class who is below and who is above [the national benchmark] and look especially at the ones just below and think 'What am I going to do to make sure they are not below next time'.*

Each teacher then identified the students of concern but the follow-up discussion of how they might best be assisted was limited and did not involve the challenging exchange of ideas. Unlike their earlier conversation, reasons external to the schooling context were absent. This progression of the literacy leader from one who apologetically gave her teachers achievement data and accepted external explanations to one who was more confident and assertive but unable to engage her teachers in a challenging conversation illustrated that more than a conviction about importance of such a process was needed. Facilitation skills of engagement and challenge were also essential and these did not come automatically in the absence of training. Even this level of focus on the data, however, was associated with significantly improved student achievement (Timperley, 2005).

The Conversations: Example Three

In this third example from the school with lowest achievement, teachers failed to challenge one another's ideas and underpinning assumptions because a strong belief in professional autonomy meant there were no criteria for judging effectiveness beyond personal preferences. It illustrates how meetings can become "activity traps" (Katz, Earl and Ben Jaafar, forthcoming) in which the purpose of improving teaching and learning becomes subservient to the process of having the conversation.

The conversation focused on writing instruction. As was often the case in meetings that did not use student progress data as the basis of discussion, teachers were invited by the literacy leader to describe their writing programs. These descriptions could have become useful data on which to base a conversation about improving instruction, but failed to do so in the meeting at this school for a number of reasons discussed below. The literacy leader began the conversation as follows:

> *Literacy leader: I just wanted to have a time where we just actually shared, had a round about the organization of your writing program. How you've got it, whether you're happy with it, whether you feel like you'd like to change it. Whether you'd like some ideas there and all that sort of thing.*

Most teachers responded to this invitation by providing a description of their writing program. All descriptions were treated as equally effective in the sense that no negative evaluative comments or suggestions for improvement were made. Teachers' inquiries focused on organizational issues and there was clearly no expectation that these descriptions were intended to deepen the participants' understandings of the teaching–learning relationship. The only teacher who requested assistance was concerned about what children should publish. She asked:

> *Teacher:*   *Do your children publish every story they write?*
> *Literacy leader:* *Yes, mine do.*
> *Teacher:*   *That's where I have a slight problem because where does the creativity, the choice, the freedom for the children to actually try something and when it doesn't work they can discard it.*
> *Literacy leader:* *Well, it does and then it comes into that conferencing time too. You see, the whole focus of getting them to write excellence is that if they come back to me with some things that I don't think are excellent – that's when we discard it and then they publish the bit out of it that is good. Yes, well that's cool.*
> *Teacher:*   *That's why I was asking – everyone else seems to get the children to publish every story they write and I don't know that I quite like that idea.*
> *Literacy leader:* *So that's cool and you don't have to. I think that's fine. If you want to keep that part, you do that. I'm not saying you change that at all.*

It could be argued that this case showed genuine inquiry. The teacher who asked the first question appeared to be undecided about the merits of publishing every story written by her students. Descriptions of teaching practice can provide valuable evidence for making instructional decisions as demonstrated in the first example. However, it was difficult to see how this conversation might lead to improved instruction and student outcomes. Part of the reason for this situation was the absence of any evaluative criteria or evidence to use as the basis of judging "creativity" or "excellence" to assist with deciding on the effectiveness of different instructional approaches. Under these circumstances, the personal preferences expressed in this conversation were almost inevitably upheld with the resolution of alternative views achieved through deference to professional autonomy. All contributions were equally acceptable. The only basis for challenge was an alternative personal preference. This process can also conceal a lack of pedagogical content knowledge. In the absence of rigorous debate, neither the leader nor the teachers revealed whether they had sufficient knowledge to judge and teach quality writing.

Conclusions

In the introductory chapter to this volume, we argued that inquiry-based conversations using evidence depend on particular habits of mind, beliefs and skills. With respect to teaching, I propose that the most important habit of mind (Keating, 1996) involves a desire to find out how to improve instructional practices for those students currently underserved by our education system and to take the risk to have existing assumptions about these students and how to teach them challenged. This habit of mind pervaded the conversation in the first example with a high sense of urgency, but was not evident in the second and third less-effective examples. In these latter schools teachers met for the purpose of improving teaching practice, but there was no challenge to existing assumptions about the students or what constituted effective teaching. They engaged in the activity of having meetings and conversations, rather than having conversations with a clear and urgent purpose.

The most important belief in the schools whose students made the most progress was the conviction that their students, although from relatively poor homes, had the potential to achieve as well as others in the country. This belief was evident in a number of ways. The benchmarks used to judge the adequacy of the students' progress from these low-income communities were those applicable to national average rates of progress. The effectiveness of teaching was judged according to its impact on the ability of students to reach these benchmarks of literacy achievement. Help for teachers was expected and accepted. Conversations about what students were not able to do always occurred in the context of how to teach more effectively. In contrast, in the two less-effective schools, low achievement was explained by external factors in one school, and the impact of teaching on students did not enter into considerations of effective teaching practice in the other.

The skills in the more effective conversations involved locating and using the relevant evidence both to judge the effectiveness of teaching and to develop ways to improve it. They were driven by a collective need to know with the evidence taking different forms but relevant to the purpose. In the first example, records of student progress formed the touchstone for the conversations in that all analyses began from that point, but the evidence from these records on their own was insufficient to meet the purpose of more effectively tailoring teaching strategies to particular student needs. The evidence needed to make this difference required a more detailed diagnosis of students' reading strategies and skills and an understanding of the strategies teachers had used but had proved unsuccessful. In contrast, in the second example in the initial conversation and in the third example, teachers' skills to locate and use either sets of evidence were not apparent. In one school, records of student progress were available but the skills to interpret the implications for judging effectiveness or what these records might mean for teaching were not evident. Evidence of declining rates of student progress was judged positively by some teachers. When the leader became convinced of the importance of examining data, she was able to convey this message to her teachers, but she did not have the skills to engage the teachers in challenging conversations. Her difficulty in doing so illustrates the complexity of having such conversations. In the other school, these skills remained at facilitating program descriptions and did not include interpretation or evaluation in terms of teaching effectiveness. Both schools left the discretion to make or not make changes in practice to the teachers as part of their professional responsibility. The question remains unanswered about whether they had sufficient pedagogical content knowledge to undertake a genuine inquiry process and that the depth of engagement was inevitably limited. It is not possible to deepen conversations about teaching and learning in the absence of deep content knowledge.

These last two examples raise interesting issues about how we think of professionalism. Traditionally, professionalism has encompassed three key features: a specialized knowledge base, a strong service ethic with a commitment to meeting clients' needs and the capacity to self-regulate or act autonomously (Hargreaves and Goodson, 1996). It could be said that the second and third examples met these criteria. The teachers certainly believed they had acquired the specialized knowledge base through their initial teacher training and more recent participation in the professional development. They were committed to meeting students' needs and they considered it their right to make appropriate decisions regarding the students in their classrooms. Unfortunately, the achievement trends indicated that they were not being as successful as some of their counterparts in accelerating students' progress. It may be timely to include within this definition of professionalism a reference to searching for and using relevant evidence to test assumptions about adequate progress and then to ensure that teaching methods are as effective as those that accelerate the progress of those students currently underserved by our education system.

References

Education Review Office. (1996). *Improving schooling in Mangere and Otara*. Wellington, New Zealand: Education Review Office.

Hargreaves, A., & Goodson, I. (1996). Teachers' professional lives: Aspirations and actualities. In I. Goodson & A. Hargreaves (Eds.), *Teachers' professional lives* (pp. 1–27). London: Falmer Press.

Katz, S., Earl, L., & Ben Jaafar, S. (forthcoming). *Networking schools for learning*. Thousand Oaks, CA: Corwin Press.

Keating, D. (1996). Habits of mind for a learning society: Educating for human development. In D. Oson & N. Torrance (Eds.), *The handbook of education and human development* (pp. 461–481). Cambridge, MA: Blackwell.

New Zealand Government. (1989). Education Act. No. 80.

Phillips, G. E., McNaughton, S., & MacDonald, S. (2001). *Picking up the pace: Effective literacy interventions for accelerated progress over the transition into decile one schools* (Final Report). Retrieved from Ministry of Education, Wellington, New Zealand Web Site http://www.minedu.govt.nz/web/document/document_page.cfm?id = 6444.

Timperley, H. S. (2005). Distributed leadership: Developing theory from practice. *Journal of Curriculum Studies, 37*(6), 395–420.

Timperley, H. S., & Wiseman, J. (2003). *In-school processes related to the sustainability of professional development in literacy*. Report to the New Zealand Ministry of Education, Research Division.

Chapter 7
Honey, Wooden Spoons, and Clay Pots: The Evolution of a Lithuanian Learning Conversation

Linda E. Lee

Chapter Overview *Issues around what counts as evidence for what purposes are a central focus of the conversations in this chapter by **Linda Lee**. Over a period of a year, Lithuanian educators worked with an external consultant to develop an evaluation system for schools educating students in the middle grades. Initially, there was considerable tension between using standardized test results as valid evidence for accountability purposes in preference to the kinds of evidence the schools themselves valued and were able to learn from to improve the effectiveness of their educational offerings. In the end, these educators satisfactorily resolved the tension by integrating the use of standardized test results with other measures adapted locally for schools' own use.*

School improvement encompasses sweet visions, practical work, and transformation through the fire of experience. This chapter describes the experiences of an expert group of Lithuanian educators who were given the task of determining how to assess one aspect of their multifaceted national school improvement initiative; the component focused on enhancing teaching and learning in Lithuania's basic schools. Basic schools include grades 5–9/10 and, upon completion, students may choose to go to upper-secondary education (gymnasiums), vocational school, or to work.

Over the course of a year, an expert group of Lithuanian educators engaged in conversations focused on what kind of evidence would be needed to determine if their efforts had been successful. At the heart of many conversations of the group was the question: What constitutes "evidence" in education? When student assessment evidence from large-scale testing was "in hand," they raised questions regarding its legitimacy and credibility – and meaning. Then the challenge became determining what other types of evidence would illustrate improved teaching and learning. Their year-long journey involved developing an "inquiry habit of mind" that allowed them to view "evidence" in new ways. Given the centrality of conversations concerning what "data" constitute "evidence," I have started with an exploration of the history and meaning of "evidence-based."

L.M. Earl and H. Timperley (eds.), *Professional Learning Conversations:*   81
Challenges in Using Evidence for Improvement.
© Springer Science+Business Media B.V. 2009

Evidence-Based

The specific term "evidence-based" arises from medical and health-care inquiry and practice, the genesis of which is most often credited to Archie Cochrane, well known for his influential work *Effectiveness and Efficiency: Random Reflections on Health Services*, published in 1972 (Peile, 2004). Cochrane argued that the most reliable evidence was gleaned through randomized controlled trials (RCTs). His conclusions were rapidly taken up by the field of medicine with the actual phrase "evidence-based medicine" being created at McMaster Medical School in the 1980s (Peile, 2004). The focus on evidence-based research to inform policy and practice in other domains followed (Davies, 2004). Consequently, the evidence-based, scientific paradigm has been widely promoted.

To complicate matters, it is not clear that "evidence" or even "science" means the same to all researchers, policymakers, and practitioners (Berliner, 2002). Shavelson and Towne (2002) propose the following in relation to education research:

> *A wide variety of legitimate scientific designs are available for education research. They range from randomized experiments of voucher programs to in-depth ethnographic case studies of teachers to neurocognitive investigations of number learning using positive emission tomography brain imaging. To be scientific, the design must allow direct, empirical investigation of an important question, account for the context in which the study is carried out, align with a conceptual framework, reflect careful and thorough reasoning, and disclose results to encourage debate in the scientific community.*

So what constitutes "evidence" in education? Without revisiting the qualitative–quantitative debate, a widely accepted view is that a variety of research methods produce evidence, and that all evidence need *not* be quantitative (Clegg, 2005; Mertens and McLaughlin, 2004; Thomas, 2004). From a program evaluation perspective, Patton (1997) has argued:

> *Using both qualitative and quantitative approaches can permit the evaluator to address questions about quantitative differences on standardized variables and qualitative differences reflecting individual and program uniqueness. The more a program aims at individualized outcomes, the greater the appropriateness of qualitative methods. The more a program emphasizes common outcomes for all participants, the greater the appropriateness of standardized measures of performance and change.*

Another consideration concerns the concept that "there are different ways of knowing the world, and thereby, investigating it" (St. Pierre, 2002). In the transformative paradigm the central focus is placed on the experiences of marginalized groups where the researcher "links the results of the inquiry to wider questions of social inequity and social justice ... transformative research has the potential to contribute to the enhanced ability to assert rigor in the sense that ignored or misrepresented views are included" (St. Pierre, 2002).

In the discussion surrounding evidence in education, it has been argued that two false consequences are frequently drawn which confound efforts to find and implement strategies that benefit growth and development of children and youth:

On one hand, a narrow and thus too demanding notion of evidence is adopted, thereby excluding, as irrelevant or as not rigorous or as arbitrary, deliberations about educational policy and practice. On the other hand, in recognizing the distinctively practical, context bound and value-laden nature of educational deliberations, many will reject completely the large-scale experimental search for evidence. Thus is created the false dualism between quantitative and qualitative approaches that has caused so much damage. (Pring, 2004)

The "conversation" in Lithuania moved from a focus on the limitations and validity of nationally collected student assessment data to a discussion of what evidence would constitute appropriate and credible "data" within the context of improving education in basic schools.

Context

In a concerted attempt to improve student achievement in basic education, modernize Lithuanian schools, and make more efficient use of financial resources, the Education Improvement Project (EIP) was prepared by the Lithuanian Ministry of Education and Science (MES) in 2001 and operationalized in 2002. The Project, funded from a World Bank loan and cofinanced by the Government of the Republic of Lithuania and municipal funds, represented the most substantial Lithuanian investment into education in recent decades. The strategic objectives of EIP were to enhance the quality of teaching and learning in basic schools and to optimize the utilization of educational funds and resources.

The project involved introducing new teaching and learning strategies, upgrading teaching equipment, renovating schools, and improving their energy efficiency, as well as optimizing municipal school networks, establishing monitoring systems, and creating education quality management and policy analysis systems. The Project was divided into four components: A – improvement of teaching and learning conditions in basic schools; B – creation of a system of education quality management; C – reduction of energy costs and improvement of physical learning conditions; D – optimization of the school network. Within each component were subcomponents coordinated by representatives of the Ministry of Education and Science and advised by an Expert Working Group.

Component A focused on "enhancing the learning and teaching in basic schools." The long-term objective was to improve the pedagogical competencies and working conditions of teachers in order to promote active learning of pupils and professional interaction of teachers. The expected results from component A were articulated in specific and largely quantitative terms which the Ministry of Education and Science had the ability to track.

- Quality of education will improve in 70% of basic schools.
- 6,000 teachers will have been taught to use new methods of teaching/learning and student assessment, instructional technology, and new teaching aids.
- 400 basic schools will be provided with modern teaching aids and virtual environment software.

- 250 consultants will be prepared to spread the innovations throughout Lithuania.
- 400 principals will have been taught to plan and improve their schools.

Component A began with a 2-year teacher and schools development initiative including 70 schools and 260 teachers from all parts of Lithuania. During this period, these teachers were involved in an in-service training program. The main content of these teacher development programs focused on teaching methods, using new teaching aids, assessing teaching and learning, and integrating Information and Communication Technologies (ICT) as part of regular education practice in schools. A network of change agents or trainers who had participated in the training program was established to disseminate the lessons learned to another group of basic schools in their regions, representing the second stage of the work. Ultimately, the intention was to make the activities of component A accessible to the entire education community. The participating schools, specialists of education divisions in municipalities, and regional teacher education centers were encouraged to disseminate the experience gained and involve the remaining basic schools in the process of change.

To support the evaluation of component A, an external consultant was contracted to assist the Ministry, their core advisory team, and the Expert Working Group in developing an appropriate evaluation process that would assess the changes taking place in basic schools. Rather than recommend a particular approach, the consultant would collaborate with the Expert Working Group through facilitating a series of workshops to identify the data and processes to assess the impact of component A. The Expert Working Group of 25 people was comprised of a mix of educators including Ministry people (both educators and individuals involved with quality assurance and monitoring systems), representatives from various education divisions in the country (such as municipal administrators), school principals and teachers, as well as university professors and staff from regional teacher education centers. The expertise within the group was both diverse and deep, including educators with extensive knowledge of curriculum and assessment, individuals with training and consultative skills, as well as those with statistical knowledge and skills. Program evaluation proved a lesser-known field; however, the group contained the prerequisite capacities necessary to engage in the task ahead.

The Process

In early 2005 I began my work as the external evaluation consultant charged with the task of working collaboratively with Lithuanian educators (specifically the Expert Working Group) to evaluate the impact of component A. During the period February–December 2005, I made four visits to Lithuania, each visit being 5 working days in duration. Prior to my first visit I was forwarded documents that provided background information on the EIP. However, my first visit was particularly important in giving me not only a deeper understanding of the EIP, but also alerting me firsthand to the Lithuanian educational context.

I began my first visit meeting with representatives of the Ministry of Education and Science who were involved with component A, followed by a meeting with Ministry personnel and representatives of the Expert Working Group including the Center for School Improvement and the Education Development Center. This second group I will refer to as the core planning team. While not an official title, they were the small group with whom I met at the beginning and end of each visit to plan and to debrief.

I visited two schools and two training days were spent working with the Expert Working Group. I came to know this group well as I spent at least two days with them upon each of my visits. In our first session I took the opportunity to learn more about their work, what they valued in school improvement, achievements to date, and the emerging issues and challenges. The big issue that someone finally articulated (or as we joked, at the time, "the elephant in the room") was the national test results that were just being released – why did students in the basic schools with whom they were working not do as well as expected? I will return to this issue later in the discussion.

I also used the first session with the Expert Working Group to begin the process of articulating the observable, measurable, or otherwise demonstrable changes that would serve as evidence of success. Given that component A focused on teacher professional development, we discussed short-term and long-term changes in teacher attitudes and practices, both inside and outside the classroom. My intention was to establish a foundation for future work by reflecting on what we would "see" – and accept – as evidence of success.

My second week in Lithuania (April 2005) was similar, in that I went on site visits and conducted training sessions. In the 2-day training session with the Expert Working Group we explored more deeply the meaning of "success" and how it could be assessed. I also facilitated a 1.5 day training session with approximately 110 school improvement consultants from Stage 1 schools. As usual, I debriefed with the core planning team, was interviewed on school improvement issues by local media, and met with representatives of components involved in school reform in Lithuania.

My third visit (September 2005) again involved premeetings and postmeetings with the core planning team, as well as interaction with other Ministry initiatives. However, the seminar for the Expert Working Group was 3 days in length. We began to articulate a two-part evaluation and assessment process that would involve school self-assessment, as well as an external evaluation process focused on a sample of schools. Not only did the group agree on principles upon which to base the assessments, but also made specific suggestions regarding sources of information, methods of data collection, and possible administration processes. At the end of the seminar the Expert Working Group agreed that clarity and consensus had been gained regarding the purposes and processes that would be used both to externally evaluate component A and to assist basic schools in the Project with a self-assessment process.

My final visit included the usual meetings and a 2.5-day seminar with the Expert Working Group, which included specific ideas for training an external assessment team, suggestions about the best ways to communicate with schools, and details on the processes for both self-assessment and external assessment. The group also worked on instrument development and even outlined agendas for the school site visits that would be part of the external evaluation process. Following my visit, I wrote my fourth report and in January 2006 provided a package of materials including an annotated training agenda for the external evaluation, as well as instruments and protocols that would be necessary to conduct the work including a set of ethical guidelines.

In September 2006, I returned to Lithuania on the invitation of the Ministry of Education and Science to take part in a closing conference and celebration of the EIP. Opportunities for conversation included some members of the Expert Working Group as well as Ministry officials from different levels, representatives from different political levels, other foreign consultants, university representatives, and educators from a variety of levels in the Lithuanian education system. These final interactions represented another layer in the process of extending and deepening learning conversations.

The Conversations

The timing of my first visit was coincidental with the presentation of national academic achievement results. The issue was that the academic achievement of children in the basic schools involved in education improvement, as measured by national testing, was *not* superior to that of children in other basic schools and, in some cases, it was lower. This issue was "top-of-mind" at our first Expert Working Group session and surfaced through a "storytelling" activity on the morning of the first day. The discussion began with comments such as "the tests [that produced the data] test learning in a mechanical way; they do not get at the heart of learning" or "the social aspects of learning are not included" or "these examinations are eager to find out only what the child knows and do not help us address what the child needs to know." The first instinct was to find reasons why the tests were not measuring what mattered, why the data were not credible.

The second layer of discussion took us into contextual explanations. Many of the schools selected for inclusion in the first stages of the Project were those schools where learning conditions were most in need of improvement, physically and/or pedagogically. The vast majority of these schools were located in rural rather than urban settings, where funding for education was at lower levels. Therefore, the conversation shifted to demographic factors, rather than pedagogical ones, which might explain the results.

Participant 1:   *This shows rural-urban differences and different social situations.*
Participant 2:   *Remember, the consultants [to the schools] have been working under extraordinary circumstances – the renovations to the schools, the days off ... we need to think about all aspects of what was happening in these schools in order to explain the results.*

Participant 3:	We should be patient. Changing styles of teaching takes time. Plus
(representative of the	the data we are looking at represent only 20 schools out of a large
audit branch	population. It is only a small sample of schools …
of government)	
Participant 4:	But what are we comparing? We need to show change over time. We
	need to assess the value added of EIP.
Participant 5:	This was not designed to assess the impact of EIP but rather it
(Ministry official	was trying to assess the achievement of Lithuanian students in
responsible for	grades 4, 6, 8, and 10.
component A)	
External Consultant:	We need to create among ourselves how to assess the overall impact
	of EIP, that's our task. But we also need to find out more about
	these results and what they mean for us.
Participant 5:	What would help us receive better information? How do we assess
(Ministry official	the process and the results?
responsible for	
component A)	

The group refocused on a discussion of the alternative meanings of the assessment data and more particularly on what array of data would constitute "evidence." In her remarks at the end of the day, the official from the Ministry of Education and Science continued her support of exploring what data were important.

Participant 5:	We feel responsible and we are afraid of it. We do not want to end up like
	accreditation, sitting there saying "this is a good school, this is not." We
	still don't have our indicators on what is a "good school" … we want to
	avoid torture and make sure we protect people's privacy, but we still want
	to address the academic component. We need to look for better ways.

Throughout the course of this first workshop emphasis was placed on the articulation of what was really important (what do we value) and how we would know if we were successful. The injection of the assessment data provided a springboard for these discussions. Clarifying purpose and discussing whether these data constituted sound or unsound evidence comprised integral aspects of the conversation. The representative of the audit branch, showing understanding of the school improvement process and injecting his professional comment on sample size, demonstrated respect for his professional colleagues in the room who had been working directly with the basic schools. Subsequently, the Ministry official gave the group permission to search for their own solutions as to how to assess the impact of the initiative while, at the same time, she did not allow the group to dismiss the national assessment data.

These assessment results were not intended to spark the initial discussions of the Expert Working Group. However, the accidental inclusion of the assessment data into the conversation provided an avenue into raising fundamental questions of "knowing." The mutual respect within the group and the permission to raise questions and explore multiple approaches – without having to generate immediate answers – allowed for the initial learning conversations within the group.

My next two workshops with the Expert Working Group continued to explore possible avenues for assessing the impact of component A. While we analyzed various types of data and their meaning, the group continued to ask: What is "quality" education? What will really measure change in schools? The Ministry already had access to a wide range of indicators (output-focused) which required consideration, the number and percentage of teachers and principals trained, the number and percentage of schools involved, the number and percentage of schools with access to the Internet and new technologies, the percentage of teachers applying new methods, and so on. However, the group argued that these numbers did not represent many of the more significant impacts on teachers' practices and attitudes, on parents' involvement in their children's education and connection with the school, and on students' learning and engagement. The group continued to explore what other data would provide meaningful and credible evidence of these phenomena.

As part of the conversation in the second workshop some members of the Expert Working Group raised concerns about their own ability to develop an evaluation process as they felt they lacked the training and the experience:

Participant a: *How do we do this in a professional manner? We don't have enough experience.*
Participant b: *We don't have institutions that provide this kind of training ...*
Participant c: *Schools have become factories of questionnaires. How do we use other methods?*
Participant d: *The choice of what to measure has to be made in a responsible way. Data can become a weapon to substantial political decisions. We have to be careful.*

The group also raised concerns about the schools' reaction: "schools think it's inspection and they are threatened by inspection" and "how do we go to schools who are afraid of audit?" Similarly, one participant expressed the view that "it is not just us who need to learn, but those who are being evaluated." So while some participants believed people in schools could engage in some self-assessment, others cautioned that "there is not the culture and teachers will view it as an additional load."

Meanwhile, some others in the group were beginning to talk about "things falling into place" or "being in the right drawers." "I start to see a process [we could use] that seems simple – at least it would have simplicity at the school level – but we have been taken through complex conversations to get to this point." These conversations refer to the process wherein the Working Group had persisted in asking questions and exploring different methodologies for assessing the impact of EIP. But interspersed with the discussions were agenda items focused on the recent school improvement literature and research about holding high expectations and fostering success for *all* students in public schools. At the end of the second workshop, comfort and understanding were operating on different levels but, as a group, mutual respect was demonstrated through acceptance of these differences and openness to challenging ideas and postponing solutions.

During the third workshop, the Group wrestled first with the principles that would guide their practical decisions. The principles included: focus on the path of improvement (rather than inspection or audit), work in a cooperative manner with schools, introduce new methods, and strive for clarity. Then the conversation turned to the practical issues of how they were really going to assess the impact of EIP. On the practical level, the fundamental decision was: should assessment of educational improvement (component A) be focused on proving its effectiveness or should it be focused on giving schools the tools to assess their own progress? While these are not mutually exclusive, making the essential decision about the primary focus affects the data collection methodology. Ultimately, the group decided on having both an external evaluation process and a self-assessment process for schools. As they developed these processes they continued to ask questions:

How will we strike the balance between these two processes?
How many schools will be involved in each process? Will they be the same schools?
How will we motivate schools to engage in self-assessment?
How will we use these processes to bring a new evaluation culture to schools?
How will we ensure the quality of the instruments and processes?
Why aren't we involving the municipal representatives? How can we involve them?
How do we assess the added value and unanticipated outcomes of component A?

The group was able to deal with methodological issues having had the opportunity to wrestle with the more abstract questions over the first two sessions without having to make premature, practical decisions; that is, they had permission to reserve judgments and live with ambiguity. At the end of the third session – now having made some practical decisions about the directions for the assessment of EIP – participants said:

Participant A:	*I see the path. It's a miracle. I see the way to change the culture about evaluation [away from an external audit and accountability focus] and I am happy. It is because of the people who are here.*
Participant B:	*How were we so silly? It's not about external people or what others said. We see the way.*
Participant C:	*We are from different institutions – I am so happy I am here – we are from different institutions but we are working together and finding a common language.*
Participant D:	*We are talking about deep things in a calm manner.*
Participant E:	*We are staying together as one family.*
Participant F:	*There are no skeptics. Everyone is involved.*
Participant G:	*At first I didn't know what we would do. Maybe I was too serious – I thought I would fall ill! But we were not in a hurry and still we managed to do everything!*
Participant H:	*You made us work, but everything seemed relaxed. And we still accomplished everything.*
Participant I:	*We have honey, a wooden spoon and a clay pot for you [for the external consultant]. These represent our journey. These are our context. We had a sweet vision (the honey), we learned the practical tools (the wooden spoon) and we have the clay pot (which the fire of experience forged).*

The third session together galvanized the group. Between the third and fourth sessions subgroups met to start working issues such as sampling and some initial ideas for instrument development. So when the Expert Working Group came together for a fourth and final time, they focused on the very practical issues of how they would guarantee the evaluation process that would address both issues of accountability and learning for continued improvement. Thoughtful questioning continued to be embedded in the pragmatic decision-making: "Schools need to be owners of their self-assessment results, what else can we do to ensure that this happens?" and "How can we best provide results to the sample of schools included in the external evaluation so they can learn from those too?" Interestingly, many of these outstanding issues dealt with the understanding and use of evidence at the school level.

In the end, the Expert Working Group found ways to utilize existing data in appropriate and coherent ways at the national level while not overburdening schools and, at the same time, giving schools access to relevant existing information. In the end, the Expert Working Group suggested using existing data, including national assessment results, to prepare consultants for the site visits. These data would enable the consultants to obtain an initial picture of the school prior to the site visit, thus grounding the primary data collection.

What were the actual self-assessment[1] and external assessment processes? First, it is important to understand that these two had distinct purposes. The self-assessment was designed to give teachers and administrators in basic schools techniques they could use to reflect on their own practice and their own school improvement journey – techniques that would engage students and parents in the reflective process. Self-assessment was viewed as a tool to support capacity building in schools and as a vehicle for celebrating successes, while the external assessment was intended to determine the impact of the training of teachers as provided by component A of the EIP. There was agreement regarding the importance of keeping the focus of the external assessment on determining the influence of component A and *not* falling into the perspective of evaluating the success of individual schools.

All EIP schools were asked to undertake a self-assessment. They were provided with a menu of possible methods and asked to use one, with the option to use more than one if they so desired. The list of methods included a road map (illustrated time line or history of their school improvement journey), a success story (narrative account of their journey with a focus on their greatest success), a photo album, a collection of children's letters, the creation of a spiderweb, and collaboratively designed posters, to name a few. Schools were encouraged to have as many people participate as possible, including parents and children, but final decisions were left to each school's discretion.

For the external evaluation process, all EIP schools were to participate through a questionnaire to all head teachers and a questionnaire to a sample of teachers, except the 32 schools selected for site visits where all teachers were to complete a questionnaire. The 32 schools in the sample were also asked to undertake the self-assessment in preparation for the site visits. A team of two consultants (one of whom would be known to the school) would visit the school. It was recommended that the consultants undertake two site visits to conduct observations interviews and focus groups. Data collection would involve head teachers, teachers, students, and parents. In the follow-up, schools would receive their questionnaire results and a two-page summary for their own use, as well as an overview of trends and "lessons

---

[1] There was also debate regarding the naming of the self-assessment process – should it be "self-assessment" or "reflection?" On one hand, having a positive process called self-assessment might help to change the "assessment culture" in schools. On the other hand, schools are familiar with the concept of reflection and "reflection on EIP" would seem like a natural process to schools.

learned" across 32 schools. Selected members from the Expert Working Group would write the overarching report.

In the closing conference and celebration of EIP, the official from the Ministry of Education and Science spoke of how they had learned from the experience. She spoke of how they had "lacked self-criticism" and now they were in a position, despite their successes, to "identify the problems that are still there." While these comments were in relation to the larger EIP, the recognition of continuous learning through self-reflection and the attendant conversations among professional colleagues resonate with the fundamentals of inquiry-based conversations grounded in evidence.

The Learnings

Educational improvement in Lithuania was and is multifaceted and complex. An understanding of the complexity was important in order to locate the evaluation of component A within other school reform activities, particularly those which involved some type of data collection. The overall educational reform initiative included four major components (and subcomponents) which should ideally interact to support the whole education reform agenda, which was (and is) ambitious and complex. Recognition was given to the fact that evidence of change as collected by component A may be influenced by schools' and communities' interactions with the activities of the other components.

The members of the Expert Working Group went through a process in which they went from questioning (and perhaps even discrediting) existing data to integrating existing data into a process they developed to generate the additional data they believed would complete the picture of component A. Throughout their deliberations the group demonstrated a high level of mutual respect as they constantly revisited the purpose of their work. Clarification of purpose existed with the group addressing the purpose of school improvement – and indeed the purpose of schooling – on more than one occasion.

Many of the group's conversations explored the question "what constitutes evidence" in relation to issues of sound and unsound evidence. While not everyone in the group was familiar with the language of statistics, sufficient expertise resided in the group to remove this as a barrier. Concerns centered more on how a variety of meaningful and credible evidence could be gathered together to answer questions regarding what was important about the impact of component A. Over time, however, their "inquiry habit of mind" – which was clearly visible in the constant process of asking questions and challenging each other's thinking – led the group to see a need to encourage basic schools' capacities for self-assessment. Thus, another layer was added to the final evaluation process.

Not always was exactly the same group of 25 people involved in each workshop. Personal and professional schedules meant some fluidity in group composition. While one might expect this to have caused problems, a core group of at least 15 were at every session. The process of "catching up" those who had missed the previous session was embedded in the workshop agenda and gave a place for revisiting and potentially questioning the directions agreed upon at the previous session.

The Expert Working Group entered the work with mutual respect for the range of skills and competences within its membership. The group then had four opportunities, each of 2–3 days, to work together over the course of a year. (Some subcommittee meetings and interactions also occurred between the visits of the external consultant.) While the pressure existed to accomplish the task, time, space, and technical assistance ameliorated the pressure through the provision of these supports.

What initially "got in the way" was a lack of confidence in their own knowledge and ability to develop an appropriate and credible evaluation process. As the external consultant, my role was to facilitate the process and provide technical support without allowing the group to abdicate methodological decisions to me. As the experts in the Lithuanian context – as well as being a highly skilled and knowledgeable group – we all needed to respect and understand our own place in contributing to the process. Another initial barrier was a concern that only certain types of data (quantitative) would be valued. The leadership of officials from the Ministry helped to allay these fears. Clearly the direct involvement and participation of Ministry officials in the workshops, coupled with their willingness to live with an evolutionary process, gave permission and confidence to the group.

A common commitment, mutual respect, and desire to see their basic schools improve permeated the group. They had time, skills, space, and permission to let their learning conversations evolve and to withhold final decisions. The pressure of the work was mitigated by the internal and external supports. They "thought together" exhibiting an evermore present "inquiry habit of mind." The process began with puzzling about assessment data and ended with the integration of existing data into a process for generating further evidence. Questions about evidence were pervasive and grounded their conversations. They kept their "sweet vision" as represented by the honey, while they never lost sight of practical questions, as represented by the wooden spoon. Through their collaborative work the clay pot was shaped and then strengthened through the fire of their experience. And, in the end, the Expert Group recognized that the evaluation and self-assessment processes they had developed would not be perfect, but they were able to "live today by what truth we can get today and be ready tomorrow to call it a falsehood" (James, 1907), as they had now internalized an "inquiry habit of mind."

References

Berliner, D. C. (2002). Educational research: The hardest science of all. *Educational Researcher*, *31*(8), 18–20.
Clegg, S. (2005). Evidence-based practice in educational research: A critical realist critique of systematic review. *British Journal of Sociology of Education*, *26*(3), 415–428.
Davies, P. (2004). Systematic reviews and the Campbell Collaboration. In G. Thomas & R. Pring (Eds.), Evidence-based practice in education (p. 21). Maidenhead, UK: Open University Press.

Davis, S. H. (2007). Bridging the gap between research and practice: What's good, What's bad, and how can one be sure? *Phi Delta Kappan, 88*(8), 569–578.

James, W. (1907/1981). *Pragmatism: A new name for some old ways of thinking*. Indianapolis, IN: Hackett Publishing. As cited in S. H. Davis (2007). Bridging the gap between research and practice: What's good, what's bad, and how can one be sure? *Phi Delta Kappan, 88*(8), 569–578.

Mertens, D., & McLaughlin, J. (2004). *Research and evaluation methods in special education*. Thousand Oaks, CA: Corwin Press.

Patton, M. Q. (1997). *Utilization-focused evaluation: The new century text* (3rd ed.). Thousand Oaks, CA: Sage.

Peile, E. (2004). Reflections from medical practice. Balancing evidence-based practice with practice-based evidence. In G. Thomas & R. Pring (Eds.), *Evidence-based practice in education*. Buckingham, UK: Open University Press, 101–113.

Pring, R. (2004). Conclusion: Evidence-based policy and practice. In G. Thomas & R. Pring (Eds.), *Evidence-based practice in education* (pp. 201–212). Buckingham, UK: Open University Press.

Shavelson, R. J., Towne, L., & The Committee on Scientific Principles for Education Research (Eds.). (2002). *Scientific research in education*. Washington, DC: National Academy Press.

St. Pierre, E. A. (2002). Science rejects postmodernism. *Educational Researcher, 31*(8), 25–27.

Thomas, G. (2004). Introduction: Evidence and practice. In G. Thomas & R. Pring (Eds.), *Evidence-based practice in education* (pp. 1–20). Buckingham, UK: Open University Press.

Chapter 8
Learning to Think and Talk from Evidence: Developing System-wide Capacity for Learning Conversations

Sue Lasky, Gene Schaffer, and Tim Hopkins[1]

Chapter Overview *The requirement for educators to meet recent policy mandates in the USA have provided major challenges for educators as they have found their jobs being redefined, in part, through an obligation to use evidence for accountability and improvement purposes.* **Sue Lasky**, **Gene Schaffer** *and* **Tim Hopkins** *provide a compelling account of the gap between the policy mandates and the reality of developing the skills of educators to meet them while continuing to run districts and schools and to teach the students within them. The conversations in this chapter take place over a weekend of professional development in the use of data for schooling improvement. In this supported environment, these committed educators learn new vocabulary and ways of thinking. Listening into these conversations, however, allows us to identify what more needs to happen for data to be used in ways likely to enhance professional learning about how to improve the quality of schools and the teaching and learning that takes place within them.*

K-12 Education in the USA has undergone significant change since the introduction of standards-based reform in the 1990s. Changes have occurred across the education system and have altered organizations in many ways including the functions and structures of schooling, job requirements of people within the system, and what counts as success. The introduction of No Child Left Behind (NCLB) legislation added additional urgency, particularly to the quest for learning from data that was implied but not as explicit in earlier reforms. This urgency arose not only from a need to satisfy the accountability and data reporting requirements but also to meet improvement imperatives. Using data for these purposes, however, required educators at all levels of the system to develop new competencies while they continued the day-to-day work of teaching and operating schools.

[1] The work represented herein was supported by a grant from the Spencer T & Ann B. Olin Foundation. The content and opinions herein do not necessarily reflect the views of the funders. We wish to thank past and present colleagues who participated in the research of the broader study, including Sam Stringfield, Janet Chrispeels, Laura Overman, Alan Daily, Peggy Burke, Betsy Pickup, Jennifer Sawyer, Jacques Smith and Kelly Propst. We also wish to thank our research participants who so generously allowed us into their districts and schools; and thought and problem-solved with us.

In this chapter we examine some conversations among a group of educators who were committed to using data to enhance improvement at the district and school levels, but were relatively unfamiliar with these ways of working. These conversations over a weekend of professional development serve to remind us of the focused and sustained attention involved in developing the capacity to use data in ways that challenge existing assumptions about the adequacy of current provision and provide direction for improvement. They also reveal how people collaborating in one project from different states and positions within the education system have learned from each other by engaging in sustained, evolving conversations about data use.

We open with a discussion of the ways standards-based reform coupled with high stakes accountability policy from the federal government have created changes in fundamental aspects of job requirements for people across the education system. We then introduce the professional development project and describe core features of the weekend before analyzing several conversations among participants. We close with reflections.

Reform Mandates

Since the mid-1990s, people working in state departments of education, districts, universities, professional development providers, and test preparation and textbook manufacturers have had to learn how to do new things. These have included developing standards; aligning curriculum; designing valid and reliable assessment tools linked to standards for English-speaking and non-English-speaking students across grade levels; developing, maintaining, and supporting large complex databases and reporting systems; and interpreting various kinds of evidence. These professionals have seen fundamental aspects of their work redefined. Likewise, state departments of education and districts have restructured, and in some instances had their core roles, functions, or task requirements redefined, to achieve the federal mandates (Datnow, Lasky, Stringfield and Teddlie, 2006). Many people in this system are being asked to develop competencies in new areas to meet NCLB and state and district accountability mandates. These include assessment literacy (Sutherland, 2004), data management and use (Wayman, Stringfield and Yakimowski, 2004), statistical expertise (Earl and Fullan, 2003), and systems thinking (Lasky, 2004). In short, the systemic learning required for standards-based education in an ever-evolving high stakes accountability policy context is immense.

The introduction of NCLB legislation added additional urgency to the quest for learning from data, in part because of the accountability and data reporting requirements such as the public disclosure of school performance, and the sanctions for schools that do not meet mandated standards. Never before in US education have schools been required to increase standardized measurable student learning outcomes in the way NCLB mandates. Likewise, they have never been subject to regular public reporting of their rankings; nor have they had the threat of sanctions or takeovers as a consequence if they do not meet annual yearly progress targets.

While the mandates for improvement are clear and the consequences of accountability rankings real, little is actually known in the field of education about how long it takes to first create the conditions in schools that foster steady increases in measurable student learning outcomes and then sustain them over time, as required by annual yearly progress goals. As the collective body of research by the authors in this book and others (e.g., Togneri and Anderson, 2003) attest, increases in elementary student scores can occur within 3 years of introducing an improvement initiative. Yet, little research has tracked longitudinally how systemic supports across a reform or policy system can enhance schools' efforts to reorganize internally over time for improvement and move all targeted students to high levels of performance. It has also not identified stages of development that schools, districts, and states organizing for such change may move through. One thing that has made this task even more challenging is that states have continued to revise their accountability systems, including their standards, assessments, databases, Annual Yearly Progress (AYP) expectations, and the consequences for not meeting them. In real terms this means that people who teach are aiming to meet moving targets, while scoring goals and ranking criteria change, as are the technologies used to meet those targets. These changes in the US education system were mandated and begun before systemic capacity to support such sweeping reforms was understood or developed.

The Project

Our project has two core components: professional development and research. It has a longitudinal, mixed-method experimental design with 32 high-poverty schools across four states. They range from rural to urban. They are also culturally and linguistically diverse. The professional development teams work with school and district personnel primarily to cultivate site-level changes in distributed leadership, evidence-based improvement planning, standard operating procedures for assessing student learning across grade levels, and organizing for improvement. Activities in these meetings include direct instruction, small group thinking together, problem-solving, and practicing with new materials along with individual reflection, planning, or reading. Another principal component is site-based guided practice. During these visits a professional development team works with personnel in each school on a specific nuts-and-bolts implementation challenge chosen by the leadership team.

The authors of this chapter have different roles. Sue[2] coordinates research across three states. She also collects data in schools from Southern and Eastern states, and professional development sessions. Gene oversees the professional development. He also develops professional development materials, and conducts sessions in our

---

[2] All names from here on are pseudonyms.

Southern and Eastern sites. Tim is a liaison from one district. He has attended all of the professional development sessions, including cross-site meetings, and has provided insight into data use concerns through a district lens. Gene and Tim also copresented the session on the data wise process.

During the spring of 2006, Gene began asking teachers and principals about the kinds of data they regularly had access to and used in their work. In many districts, participants produced long laundry lists of the kinds of things they used, while others produced much shorter lists. Our participants across all sites clearly had access to a wide array of data including informal classroom assessments, district-developed rubrics, survey data, and standardized test outcomes. Schools were not at a loss for data, though the quality and kinds of data varied quite widely. Likewise, the ways teachers and principals discussed how and why they used these various kinds of evidence in their daily work reflected a range in the ways they linked their decision-making processes to evidence. Some were new to developing a mission statement and building staff cohesion, while others regularly used various kinds of student data and other evidence to inform improvement planning. These distinctions were occurring among the districts and, in some cases, within districts. There were several contextual-level factors such as district and principal involvement, stability of leadership and teachers, staff cohesion, and availability and quality of technology that all affected the ways teachers and principals used data to guide decisions.

State and district capacity to develop data use throughout their school systems also varied. Not all states had data systems or warehouses that school or district personnel could readily access. In some states, the data being supplied to schools simply did not answer their implementation questions. Districts, likewise, had data systems of varying quality. Another key area where districts had a wide range in capacity was in the ways they provided support for schools to organize for improvement. So, while most districts required schools to have some kind of site-based leadership team, people in schools with these teams did not necessarily know how to organize or use them to systematically plan for improvement. These were key elements that shaped how participants understood and used data in their conversations.

The story we tell in this chapter is important because it sheds light on the intentional, sustained, and systemic attention people in one project paid to develop capacity using student data and other evidence in improvement planning. It suggests that before learning conversations can be held in schools and across people in an education system, particular structures, tools, and norms are needed to provide foundational conditions that can scaffold the learning towards more sophisticated use of data envisaged by those advocating more evidence-informed systems.

The Weekend

The weekend conversations came from the second cross-site professional development meeting of the project. Participants included professional developers, researchers, representatives from each school, and district liaisons. It focused on two primary elements: using grade-level teams to meet improvement goals at each site more effectively and generating a cross-site conversation on the kinds of data participants used, how they used it, to whom they reported it; and identifying tangible next steps. Professional developers worked from a success-based model to make sure that individuals or schools were not considered to be falling behind, not doing enough, or being the example to follow. Setting normative expectations was one of the first things they did when opening the weekend. These expectations were designed to be the same norms people were taught to use in their school-level leadership team meetings.

We brought participants together based on two findings from a study of high-reliability schools: when resilient and enduring linkages were created across schools focused on improvement, staff across locales became an important source of ongoing learning and support for each other; and the students in these schools performed higher on standardized outcome measures than did students from similar schools across Wales (Stringfield, Reynolds and Schaffer, 2007). In our project, cross-site meetings gave participants focused guided practice using new materials, ideas, and language. Activities were structured so that people could see teaching and learning settings other than their own, and shared in focused professional development with colleagues across the country working with conditions similar to their own. While the professional development teams provided new tools and ideas, as participants thought, and talked together, they moved each other through the steps that have led to their successes in organizing for improvement.

A primary feature of the weekend was introducing the data wise process (Boudett, City and Murane, 2005), visually represented in Fig. 8.1. The figure provided a scaffold for people new to examining data in collaborative and systematic ways. While it explains an overall process, specific skills are necessary within each of the steps. Our analysis highlights three organizational scaffolds that created the conditions for people new to this process to think, talk, and work with colleagues in their schools and across the project in ways that furthered system-wide learning. These activities served as structures for investigating and talking about data; tools such as technology or materials for developing expertise with new language, practices, and processes; and norms or rules for collegial interactions that focus on school improvement (Giddens, 1984; Tharp and Gallimore, 1988; Wertsch, Tulviste and Hagstrom, 1993).

Teacher and Principal Conversations over the Weekend

In the narratives that follow, participants used protocols, ideas, and conversation norms to scaffold their discussions about data. They took place in different settings, and show a gap between NCLB requirements for data use and participants' expertise in collaboratively thinking and talking about their data for improvement planning. The conversations show that during the early stages of learning from data, participants tended to focus on procedures or processes rather than on the meaning of the actual data. Additionally, some participants showed they could use

Fig. 8.1 Data wise process (From Boudett et al., 2005)

the new language associated with data exploration but needed more experience to understand fully what the words they used actually meant.

The Staff Meeting

One of the participating schools held a staff meeting during the weekend that involved the principal, teachers, and resource staff. They used a newly introduced protocol to provide structure for their content and process. They opened the meeting for observation by other participants so that they could receive feedback from visiting colleagues. Once visitors were settled, the principal began. He introduced guests, made general announcements, gave thanks and expressed appreciation to his staff, then reviewed the meeting protocol and norms. Staff followed with grade-level presentations. In their words, they were still learning how to hold meetings in this way, and relied on the protocol given to them by the professional developers to stay true to this new way of talking and thinking together.

The narrative that follows represents the two phases of the conversation. During the first phase, teachers shared grade-level data in response to the principal's opening question. During the second phase, the principal and staff discussed procedural information they would need to succeed with newly implemented changes in using student benchmark data to inform what they teach to prepare students for the end-of-year assessments.

Principal: *Anything you want to share about your grade level?*
Teacher 1:   *We're starting a theme for grade-level books*
Teacher 2:   *We had our data analysis meeting. We had big growth on vocabulary. We almost met our goals. The meeting was great. It was positive. Isabel is out[3] we have concern for her. We're putting together a care basket for her (almost 3 minutes on the care package—several people add details).*
Teacher 4:   *The intensive intervention class, some kids have moved up. We've looked at their data. We don't want to make it just for the new comers.*
Principal: *Are any junior 1st kids?*
Teacher 2:   *I'll do a cross reference.*

During this phase of the meeting, staff continued to talk in turn by grade levels. Each person summarized his or her recent accomplishments, and upcoming plans. While the discussion about the colleague, Isabel, was not the kind of content the protocol suggested for meeting conversations, it was clearly a topic of importance to the staff, and was the most extended conversation during this part of the meeting. It is important to note that the leading question was general, asking whether grade-level representatives had something they wanted to share. It did not indicate that the meeting was anchored to a particular school-wide improvement goal or to strategic problem-solving, but was rather for creating shared knowledge of recent accomplishments or priorities. More focused questions would be needed to elicit a deeper level of conversation.

Notice also that teachers did not actually talk from their data, but rather made general summative comments such as Teacher 2's comment that "we had big growth in vocabulary." Her description of the meeting as "great" because it was "positive" suggests that criteria other than learning from the data to improve practice were used. Overall, this evidence suggests that staff were in the early stages of holding conversations anchored to student data, because engaging in learning conversations necessitates valuing debate or seeing as "positive" talking through the implications of less than strong student outcome data to inform teaching strategies and planning.

The meeting then moved to the second phase. Here, the principal reviewed and tried to clarify newly introduced procedures and processes for using student data to inform teaching.

Principal: *Try to keep ideas for our vision. We want to complete that by noon. Reporting the student data—everything needs to be linked to cognitive planning. The district is moving toward having all schools do what we do. When you do your grade-level meetings, use the template (follow it). It can include the resource teacher. It should be to me by the 15th. I know we have action plans we have*

---

[3] "Out" in this conversation means, she will not be coming to work for an extended period of time.

*due every week. And this takes a lot of time. It will last for 4 weeks so give it
to me once a month. You can do one for the whole group.*

Teacher 1:   *Do we choose the area of focus based on the data?*

Principal: *Yes. Now because we assess every 6 weeks, our data will change every 6
weeks. This will really help us on our cognitive planning conversations.*

Teacher 3:   *So, we will have 1 per grade?*

Pause

Teacher 5:   *So if there's seven teachers in a grade level, there's seven plans?*

Principal: *Yes, or you can do the same one for the whole grade.*

Teacher 3:   *I like to see my kids.*

Teacher 7:   *So, if everybody has done their own, do we give you a copy of it?*

Principal: *Yes. (He continues) Expect for cognitive planning at grade-level meetings,
you'll always want this (holds up a resource), but also this (holds up another).
Because, yes, in 2nd grade they are looking at interventions on reading; is the
intervention being offered at the level? If the goal is comprehension—it is to
be grade level and comprehension, but to meet these, all these need to be in
place. We need to see what level they're at—is it phonemic awareness; then
we have to make the intervention appropriate. If the students differ with high
frequency words, but in intervention work on high frequency words and in
lessons work on comprehension, then is the universal access appropriate for
the student based on the data? That's when the handbooks come in place. As
you're planning your lessons, use the handbooks, teach those lessons. When
you do cognitive planning teachers need to bring data, the most current
action plan, the [name of reading product] binder.*

Participants clearly followed the norms for turn-taking, they were attentive and
respectful, and by and large stayed on task. They did not, however, engage in elabo-
rated discussions anchored to a primary line of investigation; nor did they build on,
extend, or challenge points. Questions were largely procedural or process-oriented.
This section of the conversation was largely informational. It highlights that the
ways people in this school understood, talked about, and used data were tightly
linked to the district-chosen materials, and to project resources. These tools
helped to scaffold the learning and the nature of conversations during staff
meetings, but in-depth learning from data cannot be process-bound and protocol-
bound. Rather, it needs to be bound by norms of searching for meaning and the
implications for teaching.

Along with the protocols, procedures, and processes introduced through our
professional development team, school staff were learning the language and
requirements from other sources. These included state accountability requirements,
district mandates and materials, and resources produced by textbook and testing
companies. In short, principals and teachers were being required to learn immense
amounts including procedure, process, new language of the materials, how to use and
interpret data, and then how to develop appropriate interventions or adaptations.

The evidence from the conversations among the teachers and principals indicate
that there is a significant gap between NCLB policy expectations for expertise and
actual expertise. Conversations from this weekend demonstrate that teachers and
principals in our schools were willing to address these gaps. They also used project
norms and materials to scaffold their improvement efforts. The reality, however,
was that some were in the very early stages of coming together as a leadership team.
While they were clearly working to meet AYP targets, organizing and interpreting

student data were not at the forefront of their agendas, as is illustrated by the following conversation excerpts.

> Leader 1:   *We've just recently jelled as a leadership team. Now we can really see where we are going. For example, I was able to get a great big Cat in the Hat blow up thing for my classroom. As a result of proactive planning I was able to take advantage of the sale because I knew what was coming up and what goals we were working on.*

Other schools had more established leadership teams, yet were new to developing a focused mission.

> Teacher 5:   *I noticed the school we visited, their focus, their mission statement was on the walls. My new school developed a mission statement that was simple enough and the students and staff say the mission statement.*
>
> Teacher 6:   *Our school is developing a new mission statement with our students and staff. Our school will say the pledge and follow it with the mission statement.*

The next strands of the narrative provide examples of the ways the observers talked about aspects of the staff meeting described above that they might incorporate into ways they organized to talk about and plan with data in their schools. The issues to which they paid attention, however, focused more on relationships and teacher participation than on examining, understanding, and using data to improve teaching and learning.

> *I've noticed that you're focused, Paul [the principal], and that you're pushing a little bit and trying to get your teachers to go along with you. I noticed how you complemented your teachers. That's so important and how you are able to move your team along.*
>
> *It was also evident that the leadership team was cohesive, but also the whole staff. Paul knew where each class was and what they were doing.*
>
> *Another important point is focus. In the south, we start meetings by asking about personal things, How's your husband, his surgery, etc. But it's very important to stay focused, to move forward.*
>
> *Thank you for letting us come to your school. First, they started with comments from every grade level. You can tell the focus of a principal—the data focus. Each representative had a chance to express interests and concerns.*

Our analysis in this section suggests that before learning conversations can occur in schools, other preconditions and supports need to be in place. Many of the people in our project were at early stages in developing the skills to organize for collaborative data-focused investigations. Their discussions focused on relationship and process elements such as participation and turn-taking. Whether they suggest teachers identify the features they value as important for their improvement planning or lend further evidence to suggest that they are learning to talk with colleagues in more complex ways about evidence requires further investigation.

Talking About Student Data

The next two conversations occurred in small groups as people responded to different prompts. Participants were engaged in activities during which they first generated data overviews with colleagues from their own district, and then talked from their overviews with colleagues from other districts.

The first activity was guided by the topic: "Consider what evidence helps you to improve student learning." The conversation that follows involved participants from several districts. The teachers identified the more informal kinds of assessments they used in their day-to-day teaching to assist student learning. They took turns, added to the conversation, and largely talked from their direct experience. The talk, however, was nonspecific and standards free as they shared the things they had listed on their chart paper.

> Teacher 1:   *Observations are important because with little kids … you know you can see the lights come on*
> Teacher 2:   *I think when you work in small groups, you can hone in on those students who are getting it and who is not. Then you can regroup and restructure your groups.*
> Principal 1:   *It's engaging those students in meaningful conversations, so that could be evidence. On our walkthroughs, we're focusing on engagement. We're asking the question, and before they answer, they have to put it on the whiteboard first, so you can tell from that if they're getting it.*

These participants shared what they used, while teacher 3 talked about how she used similar evidence.

> Teacher 3:   *We've done a model where we give students an independent task, and then they share in groups. Then they can see that there are a lot of ways to get to an answer. If I give them a task and I see one student doesn't get it, but another one does, I pair them up so they can see that even though math has an exact answer, there are lots of ways to get there.*

The next two teachers did not talk about evidence they used to assess learning in their classrooms, but rather about how results from their state accountability data shaped a new math program. They were able to repeat what they had been told about the product, but at this time had no experience of it or what it would mean for them as teachers.

> Teacher 2:   *Our state has put out [gives the name of the product]. It covers everything and every learner gets it.*
> Teacher 3:   *What Midtown District is doing is that we're developing a world class standards math program. Other countries are 2–3 years ahead of us in math, so we've developed world class program that will use hands on manipulatives to provide more in-depth, instead of so many points of curriculum.*

The next conversation was in response to the question: "What evidence helps you demonstrate student learning?" It took place with members of the same group and directly followed their discussion of the previous question. Once again, structures and processes dominated, rather than the evidence and its meaning.

> Principal 1:   *Data, data, data. As you guys know, you need that. So, grade-level meetings and sharing each other's data so we can help each other in instruction.*
> Teacher 3:   *I think vertical teams are good for that because you can see what is needed at each grade and for the next year.*
> Teacher 4:   *It helps to figure out where the problems are too.*

Participants clearly understood the importance of using data to demonstrate learning, and could talk about organizing teachers across grade levels to identify skill or knowledge development. At this stage, however, interpretation and use of data were barely featured. The next segment begins with the teacher sharing an example of looking at student work across grade levels. In it, the teacher focused on relational linkages and came tantalizingly close to illustrating its influence. Her comments, however, remained nonspecific about the connections to teaching and learning.

> *Teacher 2:*   *We went back and trained everyone in the writing assessment and we backed up and started at the bottom to say what skills were needed in the 1st grade, at the 2nd grade, etc. in vertical teams. I've taught with the same teachers for 15 years, and we've always had data. My principal then is now the superintendent and she always said: "Look at your data." We wanted to do certain programs but had to have the data to show why. Last year it was mandated to do [name of the product], but we could tell from our data it wasn't working for us so our principal said to go back and do what we were doing because we had the data.*

These narratives point to the importance of systemic supports in fostering the development of conversations about data. Participants were organized to talk about data, and they used new materials and norms for interaction. They willingly shared with each other, and saw new ways of thinking and doing things in action. These elements together created the conditions for trust to develop. Resources from both our project and districts scaffolded their conversations. These resources required that people learn new language and tools which shaped their ways of thinking and talking together which created new possibilities for collaboratively planning for organizational improvement, and investigating student data to inform teaching. These narratives also show how fundamental job requirements of teaching have changed immensely in the last 8–10 years.

Closing Reflections

NCLB necessitates that people throughout the American education system develop data use and reporting capacity. School and district personnel are increasingly being asked to use these data for guiding their improvement plans, and to provide evidence that they use NCLB-designated data to inform their strategies to meet their AYP targets. If these elements of NCLB are to improve education, they require people to develop an inquiry habit of mind as described in the opening chapter of this volume. Using student data to inform improvement planning at teacher and organizational levels in this way requires highly sophisticated skills and the dispositions to engage in such activities. It implies expertise in organizing structures and activities, using new tools or materials, and in maintaining normative expectations that support organic, self-generative learning conversations for sustained organizational learning and adaptation.

Yet, this kind of expertise was not a policy requirement for American school or district operating procedures before the passage of NCLB. Schools with low organizational capacity can be particularly disadvantaged in this kind of policy context, because they face challenges different from schools with greater organizational capacity. They are often at the greatest risk for sanctions or takeovers if they cannot organize to meet annual yearly targets. For these students, developing assessment literacy and scaffolding the development of expertise to systematically compile evidence of improvement becomes an even more salient priority because these skills can be key to negotiating terms of state takeovers.

Developing expertise with new tools, processes, procedures, and language all require that people have access to the tools, engage in scaffolded learning activities with them, have clear normative expectations to use them, and have opportunities to practice in their actual work setting (Spillane, Halverson and Diamond, 2004; Wertsch, 1991). Through holding sustained conversations among participants from different positions in the education system, we have gained more insight into the kinds of systemic supports that can scaffold learning as people develop their capacities for rich learning conversations. Though these linkages are still fragile, they are bridges for developing trust, shared knowledge, and a common, respectful way to discuss or debate data among people from diverse settings and backgrounds, who may not hold mutual beliefs about using student data to inform educational improvement.

Our analysis suggests that considerable attention still needs to be focused on how to structure school activities, materials, and norms so that people can develop new competencies as required by NCLB while they continue the day-to-day work of teaching and operating schools. The range in district and state accountability systems, and the resources other stakeholders (e.g., principals, district superintendents, policymakers, professional development vendors, or researchers) provide schools to develop data literacy raises questions about how much collective knowledge and will people have to build systemic capacity to achieve NCLB accountability mandates.

Policies, however, do not necessarily provide supports that develop data literacy. Yet, if principals and teacher leaders can be successful in developing site-level capacity for collaborative analyses of student data and other evidence among staff, they need proficiency in the thinking and language of investigation. They also need the skills to establish interaction norms that allow for frank, intentional, and possibly critical conversations anchored to student data that can inform teaching and organizational improvement plans. Likewise, people in districts, state departments of education, and federal education agencies need data literacy if they are going to engage in conversations which use student accountability outcomes to inform the next directions policy will take.

A key tension is that the current policy and high stakes accountability context places primacy on systematic reporting of school and district-level data to states and the federal government for accountability purposes. These accountability mandates pressure decision-making, resource use, curriculum changes, and staffing but can only be effective at the school level if principals and teachers can clearly see the linkages among policy, curriculum, and assessment, and how all these add up to improvement. These linkages are not being provided at the national, state and district level to the degree that all schools can understand, or alter, their behaviors to effect change. How to provide scaffolds and incentives for those at greatest risk of being left behind clearly requires coordinated systemic supports. How to provide these effectively is an area that needs focused research and policy attention, conversations with people across the system, along with the collective disposition and will to develop such expertise across stakeholders.

References

Boudett, K., City, E., & Murane, R. (Eds.). (2005). *Data wise: A step-by-step guide to using assessment results to improve teaching and learning.* Cambridge, MA: Harvard University Press.

Datnow, A., Lasky, S., Stringfield, S., & Teddlie, C. (2006). *Systemic integration for effective reform in racially and linguistically diverse contexts.* Cambridge: Cambridge University Press.

Earl, L., & Fullan, M. (2003). Using data in leadership for learning. *Cambridge Journal of Education, 33*, 383–394.

Giddens, A. (1984). *The constitution of society: Outline of the theory of structuration.* Berkeley, CA: University of California Press.

Lasky, S. (2004). *A policy framework for analyzing educational system effects, CRESPAR technical report 71.* Baltimore, MD: Center for Research on the Education of Students Placed At Risk, Johns Hopkins University.

Spillane, J., Halverson, R., & Diamond, J. (2004). Towards a theory of leadership practice: A distributed perspective. *Journal of Curriculum Studies, 36*, 3–34.

Stringfield, S., Reynolds, D., & Schaffer, E. (2007, April). *Four-year study and five-year followup of the high-reliability schools project.* Paper presented at the annual meeting of the American Educational Research Association, Chicago, IL.

Sutherland, S. (2004). Creating a culture of data use for continuous improvement: A case study of an Edison Project School. *American Journal of Evaluation, 25*, 277–293.

Tharp, R., & Gallimore, R. (1988). *Rousing minds to life.* New York: Cambridge University Press.

Togneri, W., & Anderson, S. E. (2003). *Beyond islands of excellence: What districts can do to improve instruction and achievement in all schools.* Washington, DC: The Learning First Alliance and the Association for Supervision and Curriculum Development.

Wayman, J., Stringfield, S., & Yakimowski, M. (2004). *Software enabling school improvement through analysis of student data* (Technical Report No. 67). Baltimore, MD: Center for Research on the Education of Students Placed At Risk (CRESPAR), Johns Hopkins University.

Wertsch, J. (1991). *Voices of the mind: Sociocultural approach to mediated action.* Cambridge, MA: Harvard University Press.

Wertsch, J., Tulviste, P., & Hagstrom, F. (1993). A sociocultural approach to agency. In A. Forman, N. Minick, & A. Stone (Eds.), *Contexts for learning sociocultural dynamics in children's development* (pp. 336–357). New York: Oxford University Press.

Chapter 9
Learning Conversations Stillborn: Distrust and Education Policy Dialogue in South Africa

Brahm Fleisch

Abstract **Brahm Fleish** *describes how the potential for conversations to be sites of learning can be undermined by those with conflicting agendas in a policy context in South Africa. This chapter exemplifies how trust and respect need to underpin the relationships of those involved in evidence-informed conversations if they are to solve rather than exacerbate complex educational problems. Instead of engaging in the difficult task of developing nuanced interpretations from multiple data sources, a single data source showing disappointing student achievement results was used as a platform for assigning blame according to predetermined politically driven notions of causation. In the absence of trust, the potential for these differing causal theories to develop rich diagnoses and solutions was not realized.*

Introduction

In the last decade, the education research community has increasingly taken on the demands to engage with evidence to ensure the effectiveness of schooling outcomes. But will evidence-based or, in a more recent formulation, evidence-informed approaches ultimately fulfill the promise of adding value to our education system? One approach that has taken a slight deviation from the mainstream has been suggested by Lorna Earl and Helen Timperley. Rather than assuming a linear relationship between evidence and improved practice, Earl and Timperley suggest that evidence, to become part of the improvement cycle, needs to be mediated through policymaker and practitioner "conversations". But under what conditions can evidence-based conversations, particularly those involving policymakers, work?

This chapter takes on the challenge of exploring how evidence-based conversations work in the political/policy arena. It does this not by looking at schoolchildren, teachers, parents or school managers, but rather focuses on evidence-based conversations that occur in the public arena, amongst politicians and between political leaders and senior public servants. I examine an evidence-initiated conversation that took place in the Western Cape province of South Africa in 2003. The chapter

L.M. Earl and H. Timperley (eds.), *Professional Learning Conversations:*   109
Challenges in Using Evidence for Improvement.
© Springer Science + Business Media B.V. 2009

examines the pathway of the conversation, the potentially productive avenues that the conversation could have taken, and the *cul-de-sac* the conversations eventually ended in. In a conversation initiated by policy researchers and program evaluators, provincial politicians began an important conversation about the underlying causes of underachievement. But rather than generating new insights, the conversation rapidly degenerated into unproductive name-calling. The key insight to be gleaned is the centrality of both mutual respect and trust as necessary preconditions for evidence-based conversations to become learning conversations.

The remainder of this chapter is structured into three sections. I begin by examining the controversy around evidence-based practice, the shift of nomenclature towards "evidence-informed", and Earl and Timperley's perspective on the debate. The second section describes the complexities, nuances and ultimately the failure of a political/policy dialogue conducted in the public eye. The final section outlines the insights and implications of evidence-informed policy dialogue.

Emerging Issues About Evidence and Evidence-Based Conversations

Few present in the auditorium at the American Education Research Association meeting in New Orleans in 2002 would walk away unimpressed by Robert Slavin's arguments about the importance of evidence-based education. "At the dawn of the 21st century", he argued:

> [E]ducation is finally being dragged, kicking and screaming into the 20th century. The scientific revolution that utterly transformed medicine, agriculture, transportation, technology, and other fields early in the 20th century almost completely bypassed the field of education.

Slavin (2002) argues that educational researchers should focus on developing a robust research culture, centered on randomized experiments. More than a research design, randomized experiments would generate the kind of evidence that could elevate educational research to levels of achievement and respect in the fields of medicine and engineering.

Within the field of medicine, Sackett, Rosenberg, Muir Gray, Haynes and Richardson (1996) offered what is possibly the clearest formulation of the concept of evidence-based practice. In one particularly cogent paper, Sackett described evidence-based medicine as the conscientious, explicit and judicious use of current best evidence in making decisions about the care of individual patients. Sackett and colleagues stress that the key is integrating individual clinical expertise with externally conducted systematic research. In their view, the integration of the two knowledge domains leads to more effective and efficient diagnosis, more thorough identification and compassion for individual patient rights and needs.

Slavin's lecture was a marker of a wider shift in educational research. Even a cursory review reveals an emerging trend of articles calling for evidence-based approaches in various subfields as diverse as physics education, education management and higher education. While similar kinds of debates about the role of science in education are not new (Lagemann, 2000), its renewed punch in the Anglophone world (on both sides of the Atlantic) signaled a new self-confidence on the part of researchers that employ particular types of quantitative research techniques.

Alongside this confidence about the potential contribution that the new "scientific" evidence can make, is a new modesty about its role in the dialogue with policymakers and practitioners. This is most clearly reflected in a shift in nomenclature from "evidence-based" to "evidence-informed". According to Levacic and Glatter (2001), the shift in terminology has two sources. First, the growing recognition of the problematic relationship between providing data for decisions on the one hand, and solving policy problems on the other. Second, the recognition that policy or practice must be informed both by evidence and more nuanced and complex professional judgment that comes from experience.

Earl and Timperley (Chapter 1, this volume) are concerned to examine the preconditions for effective use of evidence by educators and policymakers. They hope that by "listening in" on various evidence-informed conversations, both successful and, in some cases, unsuccessful lessons can be generated about the requirements for successful evidence-informed conversations and why such conversations fail. Their theoretical model suggests a series of conditions that are necessary for evidence to translate into improved practice. At the core of what they call "learning conversations" is an acceptance of the centrality of mutual respect, a desire to maximize valid information and an attitude of inquiry or what they refer to as "an inquiry habit of mind". They acknowledge the difficulties associated with these genuine conversations because participants bring with them their unique histories, values, ideologies and above all else interests. But if there are to be genuine evidence-based or evidence-informed conversations that lead to improved practice in education, individuals have to "park" their personal interests, and be committed and open to respectfulness and rigorous inquiry.

An Evidence-Based Conversation[1]

The transformation of South African education has been widely recognized as an extraordinary achievement in large-scale educational change. While fundamental shifts in deep inequality within the social order was not achieved in the first 10

---

[1] The original intention of this study of evidence-based conversations was to explore three levels at which learning conversations can take place. I had anticipated studying the internal departmental conversation that took place between the minister and his senior administrator and within the senior management (the superintendent-general and the chief directors), and between district staff and schools to understand how learning happens in these kinds of forums. Interviews with the key senior management was set up and conducted on 4 September 2004, with follow-up interviews planned with district staff. Unfortunately the provincial director of education research refused to be interviewed on the date agreed to, and chief education specialist responsible for the management

years of democracy, substantial successes have been noted in fiscal equity, institutional restructuring, ending statutory violence in schools and deracialization of middle-class schools (Chisholm, 2004; Fiske and Ladd, 2004). One disappointment in the change process was the failure of efforts to improve the quality of teaching and learning, and improve the levels of reading and mathematics, particularly for children from disadvantaged communities. While a small number of studies picked up on the problem of quality in the late 1990s (e.g., the TIMSS), the identification of the problem of poor reading and mathematics achievement in primary schools became clear both from international evaluations (Grade 3 Evaluation) and regional cross-national studies of quality (e.g., Monitoring of Learner Achievement (MLA) and Southern African Consortium for Monitoring Education Quality (SACMEQ)). One pervasive problem with the early efforts to develop systematic and sound evidence about actual levels of achievement in South African primary schools was the flawed sampling in both international and national assessments.[2] The rather general nature of the results also tended to reinforce the prevailing skepticism of quantitative studies of achievement (Muller, 2004), particularly given the history of standardized testing (Fleisch, 1995).

Addressing the most serious sampling design problems of earlier studies and taking cognizance of the new curriculum standards, the Western Cape Education Department undertook a comprehensive study of achievement in literacy and mathematics in all primary schools with Grade Six classes.[3] The study was intentionally designed to serve as a baseline, even if some of the senior officials saw it as a way of identifying schools that need immediate attention. A local university was contracted to design the study, construct the mathematics and literacy instruments, administer the tests and provide an analytic report on the results. All this was done in partnership with the provincial government.

All in all, 34,596 Grade Six schoolchildren in 1,079 schools wrote the tests. The basic analysis of both mathematics and literacy was the average grade level attained relative to the expected curriculum standards as outlined in the Revised National Curriculum Statement. Results were disaggregated by region, district and school, as well as a range of nonschool factors such as poverty, age, language of instruction and home language. Additional analysis was done to identify performance in specific aspects of both literacy and mathematics curriculum (WCED, 2004, p. i).

---

of the assessment process subsequently requested me not to use the data from the interview that took place with him. In a follow-up set of e-mails, a range of bureaucratic obstacles were put in the way of the research, even though in terms of the original plan, I had no plans to conduct research in schools. Given the need to respect the sensitivities of the senior managers involved I have chosen to focus on information that is in the public domain, i.e., newspaper statements and other public documents.

[2] Both the cross-national studies and the local evaluation's sample size have tended to be too small, given the large interschool variance associated with social and economic inequality. This has resulted in results reported with large standard errors.

[3] Only schools with fewer than 50 children in Grade 6 were excluded. A random sample of 40 children from each school was tested rather than all Grade 6s.

The report identified the "most significant" results as the aggregate performance and the high proportion of Grade Six students that did not achieve the curriculum standards in both mathematics (84% below the standard) and literacy (65% below the standard). The reasons given for this extraordinary poor performance included: (1) the socioeconomic variables associated with poverty, (2) school and curricula variables associated with home language and class size, and (3) learner characteristic variables such as age and gender (WCED, 2004, p. ii).

The university consortium submitted the final report in February 2004. The head of the provincial government thought it prudent to delay the release of the report until after the newly elected provincial education minister had assumed office. In the interregnum, the first evidence-based conversation was held around the "shocking" findings. The findings were presented to a meeting of all the provincial government's senior education managers. The presentation was followed by a very heated exchange. The response of the senior managers ranged from extreme distress to mild disdain. A number of managers, particularly those responsible for curriculum and teaching, expressed their skepticism of the assessment results citing concerns about testing design validity. The conversation rapidly polarized around those who accepted the validity of the findings and those who dismissed standardized testing per se. Senior managers from the finance and human resource sections were particularly concerned about the impact that the study would have on budgets and human resource planning. Curriculum planners, on the other hand, tended to view the study as a part of an ideological assault on the values embedded in the new curriculum. Overall, however, the provincial managers who tended to dismiss the results of large-scale testing of achievement were far more muted at this particular conversation, as it came on the heals of similar conversation that had taken place 1 year earlier when similar results were released on the Grade Three evaluation.

The first substantial conversation with the incumbent minister took place 2 weeks after his appointment. The chief director for planning and the research director met him and presented the key findings of the Grade Six study. He apparently engaged with the study's findings without defensiveness and was eager to think about the policy implications. Events, however, overtook the minister and his senior managers when the city newspapers began to publish articles about the study. Based on what newspapers claimed was a "leaked" version of the report, the Afrikaans language daily, *Die Burger*, first broke the story, publishing the "results" of the study under the byline:

Only one in six can count.
Cape Town – Only one in six pupils in the Western Cape can count and just more than 35% can read and write properly. These were the shocking results of comprehensive numeracy diagnostic tests taken by all the province's Grade 6 pupils.[4]

The story caused a flurry of activity in and out of the provincial department. The two English dailies picked up on the story the next day, also focusing on what appeared to be very low levels of mathematics and literacy achievement of Grade

---

[4] *Die Burger* May 25, 2004 [newspapers own translation from the original Afrikaans].

Sixes in the province. The headline in the *Cape Argus* read: "60% of W Cape Grade 6s can't read or write."[5]

The original department plan had been to inform the schools of their school results and subsequently to present the findings at a national press conference, but the unauthorized distribution of the report created a new dynamic and immediately created a sensationalized environment when the department lost control of the direction of the conversation.

The following day, the day on which the official press conference had originally been scheduled, more nuanced stories began to appear in the other local papers. The *Cape Times* published a story that located the poor results within the context of comments made by the new minister. Even in the presentation of the results, the newspaper more accurately showed that most of the Grade Six students, rather than not being able to count, were functioning below grade level. But the core of the story was the interpretation that the minister gave to the results, which was that the results reflected the continued impact that inequality has on schooling outcomes. Quoting the minister, the newspaper reported:

> *The results reflect the stark inequalities between former Model C [white] schools and those that were previously disadvantaged [black]. Poverty in all its manifestations is the single most important factor associated with the results, which have shown a clear link to performance.*

This adverse publicity forced the newly appointed minister to move into media damage control. On 25 May, the minister issued a public statement clarifying the nature of the assessment exercise and providing a more comprehensive interpretation of the findings. He then suggested ways in which the study would inform policy development.

While the minister's press release placed emphasis on the relationship between poverty and performance and indicated that the results were anticipated from earlier studies and the department "has already introduced a variety of programmes to address the issue of under-performance by most of our learners", the internal department response pushed different conversations. Along with the centrality of poverty as a predictor variable of performance, the chief director of curriculum planning pointed to evidence that teachers consistently overestimated the performance of their students, which suggested in her view that teachers have "not yet recognized the 'demands' of the new curriculum".

The department stressed the importance that the test results should provide information on specific outcomes, i.e., in the mathematics test on poor achievement on problems related to space and shape, addition and subtraction. The department also stressed the central importance of providing comprehensive information for each school. These school-specific reports would assist schools to assess their performance in specific learning outcomes against those of the circuit, district and province. Along with results, the department used the opportunity to push normative standards: this is reflected in departmental documents that sent the following message:

---

[5] *Cape Argus* June 10, 2003.

- All learners in the foundation phase must read, write and calculate every day.
- All teachers must provide extended opportunities every day for learners to read, write and calculate.
- All principals and heads of foundation phase must monitor that all learners read, write and calculate every day and that this is done at the levels prescribed in the National Curriculum Statement.
- All parents, guardians, family members and friends of Grade R to 6 learners must monitor the reading, writing and numeracy progress of learners.[6]

The conversation 2 days after the publication of the leaked report had begun with standard sensational accounts of children's inability to count and read. The minister's media statement and subsequent press articles began to deepen the conversation by contextualizing the results against the background of inequality on the one hand, and teachers' expectations on the other. The department conceived the evidence-based report as an important catalyst or trigger for powerful school-based conversations that centered on performance benchmarked against other schools in the circuit, district and province as a whole, which it was hoped would spark professional introspection. At the same time, the analysis of the results at a provincial level would allow for curriculum analysis of performance. The department could assess, for example, how well the children were mastering skills associated with space and shape.

When the former minister of education from the opposition political party entered the conversation, the conversation took a distinct turn. In an Op-ed section of the prominent daily, the editor published the former minister's letter under the provocative byline:

ANC destroying public education.
In the letter, the former minister accused the ANC government of incorrectly ascribing poor results to poverty. In her view, "while poverty aggravates all social pathologies, it is not the cause of poor public education". She placed the 'blame' for the poor results at the door of the "poorly conceived curriculum innovation, popularly called Curriculum 2005". Curriculum 2005 was the name the new government gave to its major curriculum reforms based the principles of outcomes based education. In the former minister's view, the new curriculum "overlooked the most important outcome of all: reading, writing and calculating".

More specifically, she argued that the poor performance must be linked to the decline of the teaching of "the phonics method of teaching children to read, which involved learning that a letter represents a sound, that sounds together make words, and then sentence and so on".[7]

The exchange in the popular press was potentially the start of a powerful public conversation, with both sides engaging with the "evidence" and offering competing interpretations based on their values, histories and theories. The emerging debate neatly mirrors Feuerstein's distinction between distal and proximal determinants of

---

[6] *Cape Times* May 26, 2004. This quote is taken verbatim from the Western Cape Department of Education's Press Release of the previous day.

[7] Published in the *Cape Times* June 2, 2004.

differential cognitive development.[8] In terms of Earl and Timperley's framework, not only was this a potentially productive conversation about evidence, but it also had the makings of a learning conversation. But as they observe, without the three critical ingredients, i.e., mutual respect, commitment to maximizing valid information and the habit of inquiry, the nascent conversation can fail.

The very way in which the evidence entered the public domain as a "leaked" report, compounded by the fact that the conversations began between political adversaries, meant that the key ingredients of respect and trust were missing. The debate, surrounded unfortunately with stale accusations and vitriolic barbs, rapidly descended into unproductive name-calling. In a unique public exchange in the local press, the minister began his carefully worded rebuttal by arguing that the evidence certainly did not support the claim that the new government's policy was to blame for the poor performance. Unfortunately the minister did not address the issues raised about curriculum and classroom teaching practices. He also failed to engage with wider issues related to the role of parents, school readiness and preschool learning, and language policies and practices. In the end, the minister dismissed the former minister as a reactionary apologist for white privilege. Once in print, the rebuttal letter effectively ruptured trust and ended any possibility of a productive public learning conversation.

Voices from the public emerged that signaled disappointment at the stillborn learning conversation. One reader wrote:

> I ask for less ideological defensive responses from public figures like Mr. Dugmore, the provincial minister of education. I plead for more humility and openness, and a willingness to acknowledge great inadequacies, even if the best-intended effort of the government at educational transformation. Let us see a willingness to debate and accept criticism, including voices from the classroom.[9]

A similar argument was published a week later.[10] The nature of this public debate and its longevity meant that the minister felt compelled to respond yet again. His final letter on the matter suggests a great deal about the nature of learning conversations and the problem of trust. Dugmore points to the potential conflict of interest in such conversations. In his view, the former minister's mind was clouded by her narrow partisan agenda, rather than part of a genuine commitment to education improvement.[11] Given the pervasiveness of entrenched partisan interests, his comments raised the question about the very possibility of learning conversations taking place in the public domain.

Interviews within the Western Cape Department of Education (WCED) suggested that few substantial conversations took place between the head office and the district offices. Letters that outlined the school-specific results were issued directly from the research directorate, without engaging the local education agency.

---

[8] Thanks to Dr. Ian Moll for the insight.

[9] *Cape Times* June 11, 2004.

[10] *Cape Times* June 15, 2004.

[11] *Cape Times* June 19, 2004.

Many of the district officials did not have a real grasp on the technical aspects of the information that was furnished to schools. As such, they were not in a particularly strong position to mediate or facilitate a dialogue or conversation about the meaning of the evidence for individual schools.

A number of schools responded to the official assessment results. Concerns from schools first surfaced around the report itself, when a number of schools complained that the test administrators were "arrogant" as they refused to allow school personnel to select the children to be tested. Other schools were angry that classroom teachers were not allowed access to copies of the test instrument. These types of concerns are indicative of the fact that South African teachers are largely unfamiliar with the basic procedures of large-scale standardized testing, something that undoubtedly influenced student performance in the disadvantaged schools.

Following the receipt of the official WCED letters with the school's performance results, a number of schools sent formal letters of complaint. Schools questioned the validity and reliability of the test instruments and results. These became important pretexts for a limited set of evidence-based conversations. The head office used the letters as opportunities to discuss curricula and teaching problems, initially through letters and then with face-to-face meetings with teachers in specific schools. The focus of these meetings was on the value of testing in providing a baseline for assessing education development and for identifying areas of strength and weakness in the teaching and in the curriculum. The province stressed that the purpose of the tests was not to compare schools, but to allow schools to gauge their own gains over time. These conversations, initiated out of complaints, were, however, few in number.

Schools, whose results placed them in the top quintile, used their "achievement" as part of their regular marketing campaign. School newsletters were filled with self-praise. For example, an elite public primary school newsletter in Cape Town included the following:

> *It is gratifying to report to parents that the test results show, in the words of the WCED that the 'literacy and numeracy standards at RBPS are those of Grade 6 level or higher'. Please accept the WCED's congratulations on these results.*
>
> *I believe that these magnificent results wonderfully reflect the quality of teaching and the effect of small classes at our school. Our focus on developing and encouraging reading and writing and comprehension skills can clearly be seen in the literacy results. In addition, parents of boys in grades 5–7 will be aware that the mathematics is timetabled for each grade at the same time every day. When a grade does mathematics, the four teachers work with a reduced class size because Mrs. Clark teaches a select group of top boys with more advanced mathematics skills while Mr. Wares takes a small group of boys that benefit from working on the basic principles of mathematics.[12]*

The newsletter also included a self-constructed log table in which the school's results are compared with the average performance in the district and the province as a whole.

---

[12] Ronderbosch Boys' Preparatory School. Letter to Parents June 1, 2004.

While the important dialogue about inequality, curriculum and student achievement disappeared from the public arena, what remained was a banal and decontextualized set of "results" that were mobilized for school marketing purposes. Popular public speakers continued to refer to the evidence from the report, "35% of Grade 6 pupils could perform adequately at the level of literacy and only 15% perform adequately in numeracy tests", as though these statistics could speak for themselves.[13]

Conclusion

There is an increasing amount of evidence to document the achievement gap between black and white students in South Africa. The evidence shows that inequality begins early in children's schooling careers, and that the gap increases with each successive year of schooling. The inequality is evident in children's vocabulary as they begin formal schooling. This is just one way in which family and community characteristics impact on outcomes. The evidence also shows how and what children are taught contributes to the achievement gap. Most disadvantaged children are not given the opportunity to study a rigorous and carefully constructed curriculum; they are also less likely to be taught by teachers with high levels of subject content knowledge. Teachers also tend to have low expectations of working-class and poor students.

The evidence-informed conversations that precipitated the publicity around the Western Cape Grade 6 Assessment Study initially unleashed many of these questions and had the potential to stimulate a major public conversation on education and academic achievement. The unique histories, values and beliefs that the various participants in the conversations brought to it could have provided a richness for further research and practice innovation. But as Earl and Timperley predict, without the key ingredient of mutual respect, a potentially rich learning conversation can rapidly deteriorate into a sterile argument in which participants speak but hear little.

References

Chisholm, L. (Ed.). (2004). *Changing class: Education and social change in post-apartheid South Africa*. Pretoria, South Africa: Human Science Research Council Press.
Fiske, E., & Ladd, H. (2004). *Elusive equity: School reform in South Africa*. Washington, DC: Brookings Institute.
Fleisch, B. (1995). Social scientists as policy makers: E G Malherbe and the National Bureau for Education and Social Research. *Journal of Southern African Studies, 21*(3), 349–372.

---

[13] *Daily News* August 31, 2004.

Lagemann, E. (2000). *An elusive science: The troubling history of education research.* Chicago, IL: University of Chicago Press.

Levacic, R., & Glatter, R. (2001). "Really good ideas?" Developing evidence informed policy and practice in educational leadership and management. *Educational Management and Administration, 29*(1)5–25.

Muller, J. (2004). Assessment, qualifications and the NQF in South African schooling. In L. Chisholm (Ed.), *Changing class: Education and social change in post-apartheid South Africa.* Pretoria, South Africa: Human Science Research Council Press.

Media Release 25 May, 2004, Western Cape, South Africa: Department of Education.

Sackett, D., Rosenberg, W., Muir Gray, J., Haynes, B., & Richardson, W. (1996). Evidence-based medicine: What it is and what it isn't. *British Medical Journal, 312,* 71–72.

Slavin, R. (2002). Evidence-based education policies: Transforming educational practices and research. *Educational Researcher, 31*(7), 15–21.

WCED (Western Cape Education Department) (2004). *Grade 6 learner assessment study: Final report.*

Chapter 10
Using Conversations to Make Sense of Evidence: Possibilities and Pitfalls

Helen Timperley and Lorna M. Earl

The education systems that form the context for the chapters in this book are all awash with increasing amounts of data. Much of the data are collected at national and statewide levels. Other data are collected in and about schools, teachers and students. The stated purposes for all this activity are typically couched in some kind of rhetoric about improving our education systems. Some advocates for an increased use of data as evidence for educational decision-making have treated the relationship between collecting data and using it as evidence for improvement purposes as relatively unproblematic. Becoming more evidence-based is simply a matter of updating our outdated systems. Robert Slavin, for example, described in an address at the American Education Research Association meeting in 2002:

> Education is finally being dragged, kicking and screaming in the 20th century. The scientific revolution that utterly transformed medicine, agriculture, transportation, technology, and other fields early in the 20th century almost completely bypassed the field of education.

When we began thinking about this book, we too were committed to the idea that evidence can improve the quality of education offered to students in our various schooling systems. We were under no illusions, however, that its misuse was potentially more dangerous than its use. We were also well aware that it was not easy to go from the raw data to educational improvement. Transforming data to usable evidence and knowledge for educational improvement requires engagement in complex technical and interpersonal processes. Evidence of any kind does not speak for itself, but rather needs to be given meaning in ways that challenge existing assumptions about what counts as effectiveness and points the way towards changing our activities to better serve the students our education systems are intended to educate. Well-constructed conversations can facilitate these processes through collectively identifying the relevance and meaning of the evidence through cyclical processes of questioning, interpretation and review. Surface interpretations can be debated to achieve deeper understanding, and knowledge moved forward by creating the conditions to answer significant questions and identify new directions.

We have learned a great deal from listening in on "live" conversations in this book about the meaning of various kinds of evidence among educators, policymakers and students. The conditions for evidence-informed conversations that we detailed in Chapter 1 have been confirmed as fundamental to effectiveness throughout

L.M. Earl and H. Timperley (eds.), *Professional Learning Conversations:*
Challenges in Using Evidence for Improvement.
© Springer Science+Business Media B.V. 2009

the conversations conducted in countries spread across the globe that are described in the different chapters. The first condition, using relevant data, requires that whatever evidence is discussed is seen as relevant to the work of the participants in the particular level of the system using it. But, as indicated in our opening chapter, simply having relevant data is not enough. It must be accompanied by the second condition we identified, the need to know more or, as we have characterized it, *an inquiry habit of mind*. Any evidence can be explained away, its relevance dismissed and the problems it reveals blamed on others if those involved do not seek to understand the implications for their own activities for improvement purposes. The third condition we identified was relationships of respect and challenge. Throughout the conversations in this book, these interpersonal dynamics have proved central. Disrespect quickly leads to the misuse of data, or no use at all. Respect in the absence of challenge, however, does not push the boundaries of accepted knowledge. Surface interpretations remain on the surface; problematic assumptions remain so. Balancing respect and challenge proved difficult for many of our conversational participants.

The promise of conversations guided by the conditions we outlined is evident in the different chapters of this book. These conversations, however, also revealed many pitfalls. These pitfalls were not restricted to particular educational jurisdictions or specific levels of the education system. Instead, they were pervasive and challenging. Listening into these snippets of conversations from around the world has humbled us and revealed "up close" how hard it is to penetrate tacit knowledge, make it explicit and move learning forward on a new level. The authors of the chapters, between them, have provided examples of both effective and ineffective conversations at each of these levels and many of them are mirror images of one another.

For the remainder of this chapter, therefore, we highlight what we learned from our collective eavesdropping on a broad range of conversations intended to come to grips with the meaning of various kinds of data and, we hope, use it to make improvement-oriented decisions.

An Inquiry Habit of Mind Is Essential

An inquiry habit of mind refers to an essentially personal quality – a needing to know – seeking meaning in a dynamic system of feedback loops. The conversations in several of the chapters (Chapters 2, 6 and 7) show that this kind of thinking can become an organizational way of being. Although this quality is personal, it is not so much the individual but the commitment of a group to engage in inquiry that develops this disposition to inquire and learn. Perhaps the most vivid example of having an inquiry habit of mind was shown by Craig – the grade 1 student who was determined to get better at reading and to learn and was not afraid to ask questions and be challenged to do it (Chapter 5). To reach such a point, however, he and his partner required coaching, opportunities to practice and time to experience the rewards of the inquiry process.

It became clear to us that some conversations among the adults, however, were not grounded in "needing to know". Even when the participants were willing, the conversations appeared to be productive on the surface but did not actually stimulate new learning or action. The teachers in Chapter 4 by Earl, for example, were engaged in some inquiry and appeared to be eager to learn but the principal had to work very hard to move them beyond confirming "what we know already" to using the data to improve instruction.

In other conversations the level of inquiry was limited in different ways. In two conversations (Chapters 3 and 8) protocols were used to guide the teachers, unfamiliar with discussing evidence, to use it in their analyses of student work for improvement purposes. In both, following the form of the formula was privileged over the substance of the inquiry and the participants were not focused on searching for meaning or the implications for teaching.

Having Relevant Data Is Not Enough

Using relevant data appeared to be the least problematic of the three conditions as reported in the different chapters. In most chapters a variety of evidence was used and appeared to match the purpose when the purpose was clear. In only one chapter (Chapter 7) were issues about data relevance and purpose part of the conversation. At the same time, there were some notable examples of using evidence to discredit and blame, intentionally misinterpreting it to support a particular case or even to stop the conversation. The case described by Fleisch (Chapter 9) is a blatant example of an attempt to subvert data being used, in the service of a political imperative.

At the policy level much has been made of the policy–implementation gap, when policy intentions are translated by practitioners to resemble something very different from what was intended (Spillane, 2004; Coburn, 2001). Coburn, for example, has described in detail how policy messages and the associated evidence are translated differently by teachers as they engage in a complex sense-making process. Policies related to the use of evidence itself throughout the system are also subject to varying interpretations. As we have noted elsewhere, it is not a simple process of looking at data but a highly interpretive process needing multiple conversations about purposes, what counts as evidence, and possibilities for use.

In some chapters, we saw the participants proceed as if they were using evidence for improvement but were not actually engaging in the complex process of interpretation that makes the new knowledge gleaned from the evidence public and visible for use. This process was evident in the chapter by Lasky and colleagues (Chapter 8) where a group of school-based educators had come together to learn how to become more "data-wise". Goal-related improvement claims were made as if they were evidence-based, but the greatest concerns expressed were about ensuring participation and sharing together with creating an undefined "positiveness". These conditions may be necessary for learning from data but they are insufficient in and of themselves.

Challenging Conversations Are Very Hard

Our third dimension – relationships of respect and challenge – requires the development of particular interpersonal dynamics. These kinds of conversations are much more than simple sharing of ideas or even aid and assistance. As Little (1990) proposes, conversations that change thinking are ones that involve "encounters among teachers that rest on shared responsibility for the work of teaching (interdependence), with their motivation to participate grounded in needing each other's contributions in order to succeed in their own work and a confidence in the others' competence and commitment" (p. 512).

In most of our conversations, the participants showed respect and consideration for one another through confirmation and offers of support, but very few moved beyond support to challenging interpretations and actions, particularly in the interests of students. Instead they seemed to accept all contributions as equally valid and avoided challenging others' ideas. Yet it is this element of challenge that moves conversations beyond superficial talk to exploring deeper meanings for the purpose of improvement.

It is easy to get distracted from the hard work involved in such conversations. Lasky and colleagues (Chapter 8) describe how well-intentioned practitioners who gave up their weekend to learn more about the use of evidence had difficulty maintaining this focus. In one such conversation, a care package for an absent colleague comprised the most sustained interaction. Other participants were concerned about how to display the school's mission statement and when it should be recited, rather than what it meant in terms of the evidence related to student learning.

In other work that one of us has been involved, we have found that collaborative inquiry is a difficult skill that teachers and even school and district leaders have not been exposed to in the past (Earl and Katz, 2006). Collaborative inquiry merges deep collaboration in the form of rigorous and challenging joint work with inquiry and is consistent with Little's (2005) reference to a large body of research suggesting that conditions for improving learning and teaching are strengthened when teachers collectively question ineffective teaching routines, examine new conceptions of teaching and learning, find generative means to acknowledge and respond to difference and conflict, and engage actively in supporting one another's professional growth. Educators may not be experienced or comfortable with these inquiry processes of questioning, reflecting, seeking alternatives and weighing consequences to promote the "transparency" of what otherwise might remain unobservable facets of practice, making tacit knowledge visible and open to scrutiny (Earl and Katz, 2006). Indeed, such a notion is contrary to traditional norms of privatized practice taking place behind closed doors with professional autonomy being considered a teacher's right. In view of the history of these prevailing norms, it should not be surprising that in many of the conversations in this book, the greatest concern with discussing evidence was to reduce threat and ensure comfort rather than to increase learning.

Although, as we noted in the introductory chapter, it is statistics that strike fear into the hearts of many people, the conversations in this volume show that it is the personal qualities of an inquiry habit of mind and interpersonal qualities of showing respect through challenge that are more of a barrier to realizing the potential of evidence-informed conversations. It is these qualities that provide the statistics with meaning and are, therefore, an inherent part of reducing the fear and ensuring sound interpretation. It is clear from the conversations in this volume that if statistics and evidence are to become an integral part of the sense-making process in education, greater capacity needs to be developed in managing the personal and interpersonal dynamics involved in the associated conversations. Only one conversation (Chapter 2) showed a truly iterative process of revisiting data, revising interpretations and developing deeper meaning. Other conversations showed glimmers of such a process. We will spend some time in the remainder of this chapter, therefore, identifying possible ways to support the development of all three capacities together.

Developing Capacities

In our view, participation in evidence-based conversations can be a high-leverage practice but it involves a set of skills and dispositions that are new to many schools. Educators, policymakers and even students involved in these conversations need to learn and to practice these new skills in order to internalize them as a way of operating. In a number of chapters, the authors have described processes to build these capacities. For example, several of the chapters illustrated the use of protocols and formulae to guide the phases of the conversations, the processes for using the evidence and the forms of interaction between participants. All these conversations occurred at the school level. While these kinds of protocols may assist groups of teachers to begin to have evidence-informed conversations, the problem with such protocols, as became evident in the chapters that used them (Chapters 3 and 8), was that following protocols could become more important than what is learned. Substance comes a poor second to process. Some other conversations (Chapters 4 and 6) also followed particular processes, although less clearly defined than the protocols used in the above examples. The focus of these processes, however, was on using the data as a source of evidence and inquiry to understand and improve teaching for the purpose of improving learning. These conversations were more focused on, and grounded in, evidence for improvement.

Each of the components, and their interweaving, requires a set of capacities. The case examples in the chapters draw attention to the importance of developing particular capacities because all too often, when capacity is lacking, energy gets shunted away from the issue and is used to avoid dealing with it. Sometimes the participants get immersed in activity traps – "doings" – that, while well intentioned, are not needs-based and divert resources (human and material) away from the school improvement focus (Katz, Earl and Ben Jaafar, forthcoming). They can also have many mechanisms for avoidance, as John MacBeath (2001) found in a study of educational leaders' responses to data. The principals in his study were provided with data collected from pupils, parents and teachers in the 80 participating schools. The data were ambiguous and there were wide perceptual gaps. MacBeath used

Freudian concepts of denial, rationalization, projection and introjection to describe the responses of principals to the data. Without some mechanism for engaging with the data in productive ways, many principals wished the results away.

Our own research and evaluation studies (Earl, Levin, Leithwood, Fullan and Watson, 2001; Timperley and Phillips, 2003) have confirmed that these reactions are not restricted to principals. System leaders, teachers and students can also show such reactions under the same circumstances. On the other hand, when key capacities are present, these reactions are replaced by ones more closely described as anticipation, excitement and learning. In large part, these differences appear to be connected to the availability of support in this new and potentially confusing part of their work, and to the emphasis on learning rather than avoidance.

Unfortunately, the pervasive belief that data can give precise, objective and unassailable information about educational activity is deceptively simple and appealing. Using data is a human activity that requires not only capturing and organizing ideas but also turning the information into meaningful actions (Senge et al., 1999). Inquiry-based conversations are pivotal to creating the shared meanings that form the basis of these actions. Getting there requires new skills and dispositions that will take some time to develop and internalize.

References

Coburn, C. E. (2001). Collective sensemaking about reading: How teachers mediate reading policy in their professional communities. *Educational Evaluation and Policy Analysis, 23*(2), 145–170.

Earl, L., & Katz, S. (2006). *How networked communities work.* Melbourne, Australia: Centre for Strategic Education Seminar Series Paper #155.

Earl, L., Levin, B., Leithwood, K., Fullan, M., & Watson, N. (2001). *Watching and learning 2: Evaluation of the implementation national literacy and numeracy strategies second annual report.* Department for Education and Employment, UK.

Katz, S., Earl, L., & Ben Jaafar, S. (forthcoming). *Networking schools for learning.* Thousand Oaks, CA: Corwin Press.

Little, J. W. (1990). Conditions of professional development in secondary schools. In M. W. McLaughlin, J. E. Talbert, & N. Bascia (Eds.), *The contexts of teaching in secondary schools: Teachers' realities.* New York: Teachers College Press.

Little, J. W. (2005). *Nodes and nets: Investigating resources for professional learning in schools and networks.* Unpublished paper for NCSL.

MacBeath, J. (2001). *Exploring the ambiguities of leadership.* Paper presented at International Congress of School Effectiveness and School Improvement, Toronto, Canada.

Senge, P., Kleiner, A., Roberts, C., Ross, R., Roth, G., & Smith, B. (1999). *The dance of change:The challenges of sustaining momentum in learning organizations.* New York: Doubleday/Currency.

Spillane, J. (2004). *Standards deviation: How schools misunderstand education policy.* Cambridge, MA: Harvard University Press.

Timperley, H. S., & Phillips, G. (2003). Changing and sustaining teachers' expectations through professional development in literacy. *Journal of Teaching and Teacher Education, 19,* 627–641.

Author Index

Subject Index

Made in the USA
Lexington, KY
16 May 2012